Showing HUNTER PONIES

Showing
HUNTER
PONIES

JENNY MORGAN

KENILWORTH PRESS

First published in Great Britain 1996 by
The Kenilworth Press Limited
Addington
Buckingham MK18 2JR

British Library Cataloguing in Publication Data
A catalogue record for this book is available from the British Library

ISBN 1-872082-75-0

Illustrations by Debbie Dunbar
Computer-generated diagrams by Rachel Howe
Design by Paul Saunders
Typeset in Palatino 11/13.5
Typesetting and layout by The Kenilworth Press Ltd
Printed and bound in Great Britain by
WBC Book Manufacturers Ltd, Bridgend

Photo credits

John Birt, 86 (both), 90; Glennis Gwilliam, 12; Eric Jones, 84; Trevor Meeks
(Horse & Hound), 19, 37 (both), 115, 117; Jenny Morgan, 42, 46, 55; Anthony
Reynolds, 23, 62, 67, 69 (both), 75, 79, 91, 101, 110, 111, 123; Cherry Wilde, 28,
85, 113.

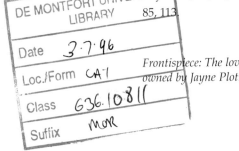

*Frontispiece: The lovely head of Working Hunter Pony Champion Gallant Lad,
owned by Jayne Plotnek and ridden by Anna Plotnek.*

Contents

Acknowledgements page 6
Introduction page 7

1 Classes and Criteria *page 11*
2 Buying Your Pony *page 21*
3 Conformation *page 31*
4 Basic Training *page 41*
5 Jumping *page 49*
6 Grooming and Turn-out *page 59*
7 Management of the Hunter Pony *page 70*
8 Tack and Clothing *page 83*
9 Show Day *page 93*
10 Judges, Judging and Marking *page 103*
11 Class Procedure and Ringcraft *page 106*
12 The Working Hunter Pony Course *page 118*

Postscript page 124
Useful Addresses page 126
Index page 127

Acknowledgements

I AM again in debt to the usual team of supporters, including Lesley Gowers of Kenilworth Press who continues to give me confidence; to Rachel Howe who transcibes my scribbled drawings into clear diagrams and to David and Dee Blunt who continue to have faith in me. Many thanks also to Debbie Dunbar for her drawings which add so much to my books.

Thanks are also due to those who provided photographs, including Cherry Wilde, Anthony Reynolds, Trevor Meeks and my friends James Forsyth and Jayne Plotnek. Joan Lee-Smith and her autobiography gave me enormous insight into the hunter pony scene as it was before I was even born and I thank her sincerely for all her help. Thanks to Alan Oliver for his comments on course building and for supplying details of championship courses.

Finally, thanks to my family for their forbearance during my journalistic struggles and to my beloved ponies for nearly thirty years of fun both at home and in the show ring.

Jenny Morgan
March 1996

Introduction

Hunter pony is a description which covers the type of animal entered in the long-established working hunter class, the slightly newer show hunter pony class, and the very new style and performance class. It can also apply to those competing in mountain and moorland working hunter classes. In theory, one pony might possibly compete in all of these classes – recent examples such as Langshot Toytown and Towyvalley Corniche spring to mind – but in practice each classification usually attracts a slightly different type.

Working hunter pony classes are probably the most welcomed ridden classes held at any show. They offer an opportunity to compete in a class where the judge's decision is partly moderated by a marks system. Since each jump which is cleared successfully gives a set number of marks, a clear round will ensure that your pony is required for final judging, except at the very big championships.

What is a working hunter pony? A leaflet issued by the British Show Pony Society suggests that he is a 'smaller edition of a really high-class middleweight show hunter'. This description would not, of course, fit some of our mountain and moorland working hunter ponies. If you asked a hundred judges for a definition of a working hunter pony you would probably get a hundred slightly different answers. For now, a brief description could be that he is a good performance pony with appropriate and correct conformation for his breed and type.

A show hunter pony, however, could be thought of as the pony equivalent of an adult's ridden show hunter. Some ponies compete happily in 'workers' and ridden classes, but generally the top show hunter ponies are a somewhat finer animal, moving more towards the thoroughbred, especially in the larger classes.

Mountain and moorland working hunter ponies are just what the name says. They are native ponies, good examples of their breed, who also jump.

Hunter ponies, then, are obviously not a breed but rather a type of pony (with the exception of the natives) which has appeared to evolve over the years. Anyone who has been involved with them for any length of time will be able to recognise a worker or a show hunter, but without really being able to tell you why!

So what do hunter ponies do? Working hunter ponies first jump a course of rustic fences, the heights varying with the different society rules. Then those who jumped a clear round, and sometimes those with just a few faults, come back into the ring for judging as a show class.

Show hunter ponies are shown on the flat, without any jumping phase and are judged very much as a show class, with conformation, movement and manners all being taken into consideration.

Style and performance classes combine the jumping phase of a worker class with a short dressage test.

The various classes have come a long way and evolved somewhat in format since their inception over thirty years ago. In 1960 a team of American show ponies came to compete in England at the invitation of the British Show Pony Society. The American ponies jumped a small course of fences as part of their show class, so the British team had jumping lessons! Although the idea of performance classes was rejected by the British Show Pony Society, the idea was taken up by the Ponies of Britain organisation and incorporated into their summer show schedule. The first classes were held in 1961.

The British Show Pony Society instituted a working hunter pony sub-committee in 1969 and in 1970 held their first working hunter pony championship. The marks system set up by the first committee ran until 1992, as did the rules regarding ages of riders and height limits for ponies; Ponies UK still use the same marking system today. 1972 saw the introduction of the nursery stakes class to encourage younger competitors.

Although mountain and moorland working hunter pony classes had been held at Ponies of Britain shows, the full section of these classes began in 1981, when showing enthusiasts Mr and Mrs Van Praagh donated £1000 to fund a championship for which competitors had to qualify at one of forty other shows. The number of shows now running these qualifying classes has risen to around ninety – a sure indication of their popularity. Ponies of Britain had also begun holding 'show' working hunter classes at around the same time. In the first year alone, they attracted 120 entries, divided between three classes.

Show hunter ponies, then, came onto the showing scene in the late seventies and were welcomed as an additional class, especially as they offered an opportunity for the hunter pony type who did not jump – and for nervous jockeys! The British Show Pony Society started winter novice qualifying classes at around this time, thus providing a winter job for the ponies and a good introduction for young ponies. These classes, which still run, culminate with a winter championship held each spring.

The Ponies of Britain organisation closed in 1988 and a new association known as Ponies Association (UK) took over where Ponies of Britain left off, thus ensuring continuity of all classes – and the introduction of new ones. 1985 saw the introduction of style and performance classes, and 1994 witnessed the first Helen Forsyth Style and Performance Championship. The National Pony Society also holds both open and novice mountain and moorland working hunter pony qualifying classes with the open final being held at the Horse of the Year Show for the last few years.

1995 saw the start of winter qualifying classes for mountain and moorland ponies, under Ponies UK rules, and no doubt the future will bring even more new classes. One thing can be sure: if you have a good hunter pony, there will never be a shortage of classes you can compete in.

The huge entries in all of these classes are a certain sign of their popularity – and at least for the classes which have a marks system, some of the results are not solely reliant on the judge's opinion!

CHAPTER ONE

Classes and Criteria

I F SHOWING hunter ponies appeals to you, the first thing to do is work out which class(es) you want to compete in. The following list will give you a general guide to the classes on offer. Do bear in mind, though, that rules as well as age and height limits do change from time to time – those quoted below are correct for 1996. Always consult the current rule book of your chosen society to be absolutely sure what is required for each class.

WORKING HUNTER PONY CLASSES

Cradle stakes

This class is also sometimes called Beginners Stakes; it is a working hunter pony class for the smallest children and their ponies. The fences are small and should be designed to encourage and not to test. It is rare to find serious hazards such as banks or water in this class.

Cradle stakes ponies are very often natives, with many being Welsh Section A or B. They should be calm and sensible but also willing. There are far more refusals in this class than in any other, possibly because small ponies learn full well how to take advantage of their small riders. However, there are many genuine schoolmasters around who are able to give a child a safe and successful introduction to working hunter pony classes. This type of pony is often an old family favourite and may well be available on loan – if you put your name down early enough.

Even if his conformation is not top class, a cradle stakes pony may do well if he jumps a nice clear round, because his manners

11

*Cradle stakes
pony Aston
Tinkerbell,
ridden by Sarah
Gwilliam.*

Cradle stakes pony Aston Tinkerbell, ridden by Sarah Gwilliam.

will give him good marks. It is quite acceptable for a cradle stakes pony to trot between some of his fences and around the corners. However, he should canter as well and take the majority of fences from a canter. He will be required to gallop only in his individual show.

British Show Pony Society rules for cradle stakes classes are: 'Mare or gelding, four years old or over, not exceeding 12hh. Riders not to have attained their tenth birthday before 1st January in the current year'. For British Show Pony Society classes the height of fences is 1ft 9in. minimum and 2ft 3in. maximum; spread to be 1ft 6in. minimum and 2ft 6in. maximum. It is not advisable for coursebuilders to use a bullfinch in cradle stakes classes, and not all fences should be at the maximum height. Water must be only natural (not coloured) and in some kind of container. Polythene sheets and imitation water are not recommended.

Under Ponies UK rules this class is called Beginners Stakes and the height of the fences is 1ft 9in. minimum and 2ft 6in. maximum; the maximum spread being 2ft 6in. The height and age limits for the ponies are as in British Show Pony Society classes but riders are not to have attained their eleventh birthday before the 1st January in the current year.

Nursery stakes

This is the second level of competition with slightly bigger ponies and older children, although some ponies and riders do combine this with cradle stakes. Under current British Show Pony Society rules, the winner of the cradle stakes at any show cannot compete in novice or open nursery stakes at the same show, so do check the latest rules if you think this could apply to you. The fences will be slightly higher, and the nursery stakes pony needs to be more active in his jumping round. He should canter between the fences (unless there is a difficult corner or change of leg) and he will usually be required to gallop, sometimes after his individual show on his own or in groups of up to four together. Nursery stakes ponies move away slightly from the native and towards the native-cross 'blood' pony, but should still retain the substance of a hunter.

Under British Show Pony Society rules nursery stakes are for: 'Mare or gelding, four years old or over, not exceeding 13hh. Riders not to have attained their twelfth birthday before 1st January in the current year'. Under British Show Pony Society rules, the height of the fences is 2ft minimum and 2ft 6in. maximum; the permitted spread being 1ft 9in. minimum and 2ft 9in. maximum. There must be some definite change of course between the cradle and nursery stakes classes, and again bullfinches are not recommended.

Under Ponies UK rules, the heights of the fences are the same, as are the height of pony and the age of the rider.

Open working hunter pony

These are the classes for older children and larger ponies and are usually divided into different height and age sections. The ideal pony will be a proportionately smaller version of a middle-weight hunter. He tends to be bred specifically for the job, although some pure-bred natives compete successfully in these classes under British Show Pony Society and Ponies UK rules. There will (hopefully) be a good course of natural fences, which will have to be jumped competently with fluency and style. Competition in these classes is very strong and ponies with conformation faults or lack of jumping ability will not make it to the top. 13hh and 14hh ponies may be galloped together in groups of not more than four and larger ponies may be galloped all together.

Height and age limits and specific rules are as follows:

13hh section

British Show Pony Society rules say: 'Mare or gelding, four years old and over, not exceeding 13hh. Riders not to have attained their fourteenth birthday before 1st January in the current year'. The height limits for fences are 2ft 6in. minimum and 3ft maximum; spreads being 2ft 3in. minimum and 3ft 3in. maximum. There has to be a change of course between the nursery stakes and the 13hh open working hunter pony class. A water jump must not exceed 6ft in width, and a white tape or lath must be provided for the landing side. 13hh ponies may jump a bullfinch but the frame of the fence must not exceed the maximum permitted height. 13hh ponies may be galloped individually or four at a time.

In Ponies UK classes, fence height limits are the same, but the permitted maximum spread is 3ft 3in. Riders' age limits are the same.

14hh section

British Show Pony Society rules stipulate: 'Mare or gelding, four years old or over, exceeding 13hh but not exceeding 14hh. Riders not to have attained their sixteenth birthday by 1st

January in the current year. Height of fences is 2ft 9in. minimum and 3ft 3in. maximum with a minimum spread of 2ft 9in. and a maximum spread of 4ft. The maximum width for water is 8ft. 14hh ponies may be galloped individually or four at a time.

Under Ponies UK rules for this class, the rider must not have attained their seventeenth birthday before January 1st in the current year.

Lemington Katinka, owned by Jayne Plotnek and ridden by Anna Plotnek, demonstrating excellent style over a typical working hunter pony fence.

15hh section

British Show Pony Society rules say: 'Mare or gelding, four years old or over, exceeding 14hh but not exceeding 15hh. Riders not to have attained their eighteenth birthday before 1st January in the current year.' Height of fences is 3ft minimum and 3ft 9in. maximum. Spreads are 3ft 6in. minimum and 4ft 6in. maximum. Water can be up to 10ft wide. 15hh ponies can be galloped all together.

Under Ponies UK rules the age of riders is 'not to have attained their twentieth birthday before 1st January in the current year'.

15

Intermediate class

Currently only the British Show Pony Society runs this class and its rules say, 'Mare or gelding, four years old or over, exceeding 14.2hh and not exceeding 15.2hh. Riders who are under eighteen years of age must be Intermediate Members and those up to and including twenty-five years must be Showing Members'. The age limits are: 'Riders must have attained their sixteenth birthday but not their twenty-fifth birthday before the 1st January in the current year'.

Fences are exactly the same as for the 15hh class, as is water.

Ponies UK do not run this class, but it should be noted that their age limit is higher for the 15hh section.

Novice working hunter pony

These are for the younger or less experienced pony and therefore there are restrictions as to who can enter. You should always check your eligibility carefully with the show schedule and the rules handbook. Generally speaking any pony which has won an open class under the same rules would not be considered a novice, but do check carefully. Some rules call for the pony to be shown in a snaffle bridle. If a novice pony were to trot in the middle of a double, he would not normally be penalised for it as long as he cantered when approaching his other fences.

The height and spread of fences for novice classes is generally 6in. less than for open classes. The age of rider and the height of pony is the same. In a mixed height novice class the course will be altered between sections and each pony and rider must be the correct age/height for their section. All ponies have to be four years old and over. A novice working hunter pony is one that has not won a first prize of £5 or over, prior to 1st October in the previous year, in a British Show Pony Society affiliated class. If it wins a novice class, it remains a novice until 30th September, no matter how many novice classes it may win. The only exceptions to the prize-money rule are for ponies who win show pony, show hunter, and unaffiliated classes. Ponies who win open cradle or nursery stakes classes can still be a novice in the 13hh class until they win an open class.

Under Ponies UK rules, a novice working hunter pony is one which has not won a first prize of £5 or more at ANY show on or before the 1st October in the previous year.

Mountain and moorland working hunter pony

These classes are for registered native ponies only, and classes are either split by breed or by height of pony. They must be five years old or over and registered in the main body of their stud book. Mares with a living foal born during the current year and ponies who have won more than £100 under BSJA rules are not eligible. All ponies are shown in their natural state and unplaited.

Under National Pony Society rules, the classes are divided into three sections.

- Section 1 is for ponies not exceeding 12.2hh. The height of the fences is 2ft minimum and 2ft 3in. maximum, with a maximum spread of 2ft.

- Section 2 is for ponies exceeding 12.2hh but not exceeding 13.2hh. The height of the fences is 2ft 3in. minimum and 2ft 9in. maximum, with a maximum spread of 2ft 6in.

- Section 3 is for ponies exceeding 13.2hh but not exceeding 14.2hh. Welsh Cobs over 14.2hh may enter the class but not qualify for any finals. The height of the fences is 2ft 9in. minimum and 3ft 3in. maximum, with a maximum spread of 3ft 3in.

Under Ponies UK rules the classes are divided differently. There are two sections, small breeds and large breeds: the small breeds class is for Welsh Section B, Shetland, Dartmoor, Exmoor and Welsh Section A; the large breeds class is for Highlands, Fells, Dales, New Forest, Connemara, and Welsh Sections C and D.

Occasionally the Welsh Section B ponies have a section of their own.

The heights of fences are as follows: small breeds – minimum 2ft; maximum 2ft 3in.; spread 2ft 3in. Welsh Section B (if judged separately) – minimum 2ft 3in.; maximum 3ft; spread 3ft. Large breeds – minimum 2ft 6in.; maximum 3ft 3in.; spread 3ft 3in. Novice classes are 3in. lower for the small breeds and 9in. lower for the large breeds.

Style and performance

These classes were started by Ponies UK and tend to be mostly run under their rules. The rules for eligibility (regarding height of pony and rider's age) tend to be the same as for open working hunter pony classes. Under Ponies UK rules the height of the fences, even in an open style and performance class, must not exceed the height limit for novice working hunter classes.

In these classes, greater emphasis is placed on the way a pony goes and jumps; the marks being allotted accordingly. No marks are allotted for conformation. The jumping round is exactly as in an ordinary working hunter pony class, but the ridden show is either a freestyle performance, encompassing set movements, or a set pattern.

SHOW HUNTER PONY CLASSES

The show hunter pony is usually – although not always – a finer type with more 'blood'. He is required only to do a ridden show and not to jump, so he is not given marks as such, but assessed by the judge in comparison to the other competitors in the class.

Lead rein pony of show hunter type

Under both British Show Pony Society and Ponies UK rules, this is open to a mare or gelding, four years old and over, not exceeding 12hh, to be ridden by a rider who has not attained their eighth birthday by the 1st January in the current year. The pony is to be led by an attendant and shown in a snaffle bridle.

12hh show hunter pony

Under British Show Pony Society and Ponies UK, this is open to a mare or gelding, four years old or over, not exceeding 12hh. Riders not have attained their eleventh birthday before 1st January in the current year.

13hh show hunter pony

Mare or gelding, four years old or over, exceeding 12hh but not exceeding 13hh. Riders not to have attained their fourteenth

A good show hunter pony type – Clinwil Diplomat, ridden by Fiona Lintott.

birthday before 1st January in the current year – according to both British Show Pony Society and Ponies UK rules.

14hh show hunter pony

Mare or gelding, four years old or over, exceeding 13hh but not exceeding 14hh. Riders not to have attained their sixteenth birthday before 1st January in the current year (British Show Pony Society), or their seventeenth birthday etc. (Ponies UK).

15hh show hunter pony

Mare or gelding, four years old or over, exceeding 14hh but not exceeding 15hh. Riders not to have attained their eighteenth birthday before 1st January in the current year (British Show Pony Society), or their twentieth birthday etc. (Ponies (UK)).

Intermediate classes

For intermediate classes held under the British Show Pony Society rules, the age limits and height of pony are as for working hunter classes.

Important: It has to be reiterated that these rules and fence heights are quoted only for guidance. Although rules do not alter very often, they CAN change. You must always read the current rule book carefully before taking part in any class.

CHAPTER TWO

Buying Your Pony

ONCE YOU have worked out exactly which class(es) you want to compete in, the next thing to decide is at what level, because you will want to buy a pony who can fulfil your aims. If you are ambitious and want to qualify for the finals of various championships then you will have to start with a pony that is capable of being placed at top level. A 'ready made' pony of that calibre will cost a great deal of money. You should also remember that just because a pony has done well for his previous owners, he may not do as well for you. They may be more experienced at producing ponies or their rider may have a better relationship with the pony. Sometimes a rider and a pony just do not 'get on' despite every effort, and it is better then to change ponies and avoid much frustration.

Even a pony with 'potential' will probably not come cheap. However, if you just want to compete at local level, with perhaps some Pony Club activities or hunting thrown in, then your pony may well be less expensive and easier to find. Often parents are far too ambitious on their child's behalf. If you buy a pony which has done a lot of winning but perhaps is too much for your child to ride, you risk a transfer of affection from riding to some other hobby, and very quickly. Do remember that it takes younger children in particular, a long time to form a partnership with their pony. Do not expect miracles in the first few weeks or even months. The pony will be used to a different rider and may take time to settle in a new home. For this reason it is often better to buy open working hunter ponies at the end of a season so that the new team has plenty of time to get used to each other before the next showing season.

Although some ponies compete successfully in both show hunter and worker classes or one of those and native classes, you may have to choose one or the other. The best examples of 'dual' or 'multi-purpose' ponies are as follows:

• **Welsh Section A** • **Small Section B** • **Some Dartmoors**
Cradle stakes, possibly also nursery stakes. Some of these ponies make lead rein or 12hh show hunter ponies.

• **Welsh Section B** • **Small New Forest** • **Some Dartmoors**
Nursery stakes. Often Welsh Section B ponies can compete in show hunter pony classes.

• **Welsh Section B** • **New Forest** • **Small Connemara**
13hh classes and possibly show hunter.

• **Welsh Section B** • **Lightweight Welsh Section C**
• **New Forest** • **Connemara**
14hh classes.

• **Connemara**
15hh, and show hunter possibly.

Obviously a Welsh Section C or D would not be suitable for show hunter classes (being too heavily built), and only a fine Section C could do workers. He might then, of course, be too light for mountain and moorland classes.

You will need to consult the rule book to ensure that your child is not going to be out of the class that the pony is in at the end of the season, which will of course be just as they have got going together! If your child is very big for his or her age, you may need to move up a height bracket before it would be strictly necessary, to get the right picture. Mountain and moorland ponies can be ridden by anyone, of any age, but obviously a very big person on a very small pony does not look right.

The decision as to whether to buy an older, more experienced pony or a young one can be influenced by many factors. If you have a child who is nervous of jumping, it would not be sensible to buy a young pony who may stop or jump badly if the course is tricky. This will only frighten the child and may well ruin the pony. This child needs a schoolmaster, who would usually be bought privately, often from an advertisement in a publication such as *Horse and Hound*, or, if you are lucky enough, by word of mouth. This kind of pony is often a well-loved

A nice type of child's pony with a snaffle mouth, taking a jump very confidently for his young rider.

family friend and may be available for loan, if his family cannot bear to part with him altogether. If you do loan a pony, make sure that you have a proper written agreement and that the pony is adequately insured. Never, ever make such agreements verbally, even with people that you know really well.

If your rider is reasonably experienced or you are an adult taking up mountain and moorland classes, you can have a great deal of fun bringing on a novice hunter pony. The British Show Pony Society runs a winter season of novice classes culminating in a spring championship show. The native societies are in the process of following suit.

There has been a recent increase in the number of hunter pony in-hand classes, which are for the one-, two- or three-year-old pony likely to make a hunter pony at maturity. If you have the space, the time and the patience, you might be able to buy a very good pony at a lower price if you can find a youngster who has had success in these classes. There is a great deal of satisfaction to be gained from bringing on a young pony – but remember to do your sums so that the height of the pony, say, at five or six years will be right for the age of your rider then.

With the high standards in competition today, there is no point in buying a pony with poor conformation. If you are inexperienced, you should study this subject or trust the advice of a knowledgeable friend. A pony can be the best jumper ever, but whatever rules you are competing under (with the exception of those governing style and performance classes) he will not do well unless he has good conformation and is the right 'type' for his class. However, the converse of this is that if he does not jump, you may as well forget him also. You have to get round the course with no faults (or at least minimal faults) to be in with a chance.

There are some things that you can change, but never the basic frame shape and to some degree the action. A weedy neck, for example, can be built up, and action does improve with increased strength and fitness, but something like a dipped back can never be altered.

With the publication of show results, it is possible to know the reputation of most ponies who are regularly competing, before you see them advertised, but it is important to remember that just because a certain pony has done well for his current owners, it might not do so well for you, just as it is not always possible to pass a pony down to members of the same family. It is not worth the struggle if the partnership is not there.

Very few working hunter ponies of any merit appear in auction sales, apart from a few in the National Pony Society Annual Sales or in native breed society sales. If you do intend to try and buy your pony this way, be aware that there are certain conditions which apply to animals purchased in a sale. If they are warranted sound and free from vice, then this is a guarantee. You must have the cash to pay for your purchase at the time of the sale, and you should have a headcollar and travelling kit and some pre-arranged method of transporting him home. Although there are usually transporters at the sales, their charges are very high and the pony might have to stand on the lorry for many hours, whilst others are delivered.

This method of purchase is only for the confident – I wish I had a pound for every pony I brought back from a sale because

I felt sorry for it! You must set yourself a limit for spending and not go above it. If you intend to buy a certain pony and want to pay the auctioneers with a cheque, you must ask your bank to contact the auctioneer's bank beforehand to make the necessary arrangements. You should insure the pony immediately, either on a temporary certificate from the auctioneers or through your usual insurers. If you don't, you can be sure the pony will lame itself, or worse, on the journey home. Every pony that I have ever bought from a sale has 'coughed' shortly afterwards. Whether it is the stress of the experience, the draughty sale yard or being in close proximity to a number of strangers, one cannot be sure. If you can keep him away from other ponies for a week or two, then this is a good idea.

Do ensure that you get all the relevant papers from the auctioneer or a written guarantee that they will be forwarded later. A registered pony is always worth more than an unregistered one and if he later turns out not to have papers, you can take action against the auctioneers. If you have no proof, then it may be impossible to get later.

If you are inexperienced it is important to learn as much as you can about what you want, before you part with your cash. Go to the county shows and watch the classes. The marks sheets are usually displayed at the secretary's office after the class. Look at the marks of the ponies that YOU liked and see where they did well or badly. You can learn a great deal from this. Never be afraid to ask the advice of more experienced exhibitors. Most will give you the benefit of their advice, but not whilst they are busy in the collecting ring! There are now a number of videos available from the various societies, which will also give you guidance.

The most usual route to purchase is through a private advertisement. These appear in their hundreds every week in *Horse and Hound* and similar publications. You will know what your budget can stretch to and will have made the decisions as to size, age and so on and you can then study what is on offer. When you arrange to view a pony, there are several important questions that you should always ask:

1 Is the pony good to catch/load/shoe/clip/in traffic? A pony who is not good in traffic will be a nuisance on a showground, even if he does not have to go on the roads at home. Even if you do not want him shod, he will have to have his feet trimmed regularly and this should be considered. Any pony which is difficult to load should be disregarded immediately. There is nothing worse than being late for a show because you have been doing the 'lungeing rein and broom dance' in your drive at home.

2   Does he have any vices – windsucking, crib-biting, box walking etc.? It is an offence under Trades Description legislation to sell a pony with any vice and not declare this to prospective purchasers. Having said this, many good ponies do have vices – one of my best ponies ever is a windsucker – and if you know what you are getting, it is not always a bar to purchase. It can be a way that a pony calms himself down before a competition – a bit like an adult having a cigarette or a drink – and if this is the case, some otherwise nervous ponies can be good competitors. Box walking and weaving can put strain on the joints. However, both of these vices happen less or not at all when the pony is in the field, so keeping him out most of the time coupled with maybe stabling him in a big barn, if such a thing is available, may mean that if everything else is right with the pony, these vices may not matter too much.

3   Does he have any history of laminitis or other health problems? Past episodes of laminitis can often be seen in the hoof growth, but this need not be a barrier to purchase, if you have the knowledge and facilities to manage this condition. Often older, schoolmaster ponies have this problem, but the extra care needed to look after them is outweighed by their value in giving your child experience and confidence. Chronic obstructive pulmonary disease (COPD) is another common problem these days but with the easy availability of dust-free bedding and haylage products, it is a relatively easy condition to manage. It goes without saying, that one would only tolerate one of these problems, if the pony was absolutely right in every other way. Poor feet can be a real nuisance for a working hunter pony. If he loses shoes easily because his feet are crumbly, you can guarantee he will do this just before a show at the time when the blacksmith is on holiday. If there are lots of rows of nail holes in the feet, you should be suspicious. It means he has been shod often – ask why this is. Although it is rare to do things such as firing to ponies' legs, it may be done to bigger ponies and the marks would usually be very clear on the legs. Don't even consider a pony with evidence of treatment like this.

4 Why are you selling him? This is sometimes the million-dollar question if a pony has in some way proved unsuitable for the present owners. If the rider has outgrown the class, however, and there do not appear to be any younger brothers and sisters, then this can be a good sign. There are all kinds of reasons, in between these two, and if you feel uneasy about the answer given then you will need to give the whole matter more careful consideration. As has been said before, some riders and ponies just do not gel, through no fault of either party. If the owners tell you that this is the case, they may be prepared to let you have a short trial, to ensure that history doesn't repeat itself with your rider. In these circumstances, the pony should be kept stabled and adequately insured.

When you go to look at a potential purchase, you must allow enough time for a thorough trial. Be suspicious of the pony who is already tacked up when you get there (he might be difficult to catch, groom or tack up). If the pony is sweaty or looks tired, he may well have been ridden before your arrival. It is therefore always reassuring to see the pony caught up from the field and made ready for you whilst you are there. Bear in mind that an unscrupulous vendor could have got up at 5 a.m. to take the little perisher for a ten-mile hack and then hosed him down afterwards – and you would never know! Beware of the pony who seems to be nervous of his usual handler. He may well have been beaten into good behaviour and may recover his difficult tendencies, whatever they were, when he realises he is in a different home.

You should always ask to see the pony trotted out in hand first. The surface should be as level as possible and preferably a hard surface, such as concrete. You should look carefully to see that he is sound, level and straight in his movement. Any deviation from this, such as dishing or plaiting, will be marked down in the ring. He is better trotted fairly slowly, but not so slowly that it hides his true movement. If the owner trots him up at a ridiculously fast speed, so you can't see anything at all, then ask them to do it more slowly. Remember, you are the (potential) customer and therefore have the right to take a careful look at the goods on offer.

Check over his conformation (see Chapter 3) as he stands in front of you and look also at the whole picture. Is he a 'smiley' sort of pony? Does he catch the eye – even if he is 'in the rough'?

A working hunter pony should be a careful and willing jumper.

See how he behaves with his regular handler. Is he relaxed and happy? Does he fidget – or even try to bite? How does he behave when he is tacked up?

You should see him ridden first and then your jockey should ride. There should be a safe area for your child to ride in, preferably a manege. If you have any misgivings about the pony, or if he looks too strong or unruly when ridden by the owner, don't put your child on board. Never, ever let your child go out on the road on a strange pony, no matter how quiet his owner says he is. My daughter spent a week in intensive care after a fall from a '100% safe schoolmaster' who bolted with her along the road and into a car. The owner is trying to sell you the pony and some unscrupulous people will tell you anything.

You should remember that the jumps in the pony's field are the ones that he sees and jumps regularly. If possible, change the jumps around so that you can check whether he is troubled by a different fence.

If your child hates the pony, there will never be any chance of success. However good the pony, you would wasting your time to buy it.

If you are unsure about whether or not to purchase, any genuine owner will let you come back a second time. If your child has lessons from someone, or if you have a more experienced friend, then take them with you to see the pony. Two opinions are always better than one.

Beware of the seller who tries to give you a veterinary certificate issued by his own vet. You must have your own vetting done by an independent vet. Often, this certificate will be needed for insurance anyway. If it is an older pony, you may well consider it a good investment to have the feet and lower limbs x-rayed.

If you want to take part in top-class show hunter classes then no lumps or bumps or visible scars must be present. For a worker, some judges will tolerate splints and other signs of wear and tear, but others will not. One very well-known working hunter pony has scars on his knees from a fall on the road, and he is a good example of how judges' opinions can vary. Some judges take no notice at all of his scars, while others will put him down the line for them, despite the fact that he an extremely nice pony. I have known some very well-regarded ponies who have won top championships whilst sporting splints or windgalls, and I have seen judges put a good pony out of contention because of a small scar. Obviously if your pony has no blemishes at all, this is the best situation to be in. If your potential purchase has a mark or a lump, then you have to decide whether you want to accept this or not.

Some vendors may let you have the pony on trial for a few days or let your jockey ride him at a show. If you do take a pony on trial without paying for him, you should always arrange adequate insurance and keep him stabled whilst on your premises.

You should always have a written receipt from the vendor and make sure that you are given all the necessary breed society and other papers. If the pony is vaccinated, you should ask for the certificate and check that it is up to date. If you are buying a novice pony specifically for novice classes you can check with the British Show Pony Society that it really does qualify. If you are buying an open pony, the Society will also have a record of its successes.

It may be that the owner wants to sell the tack with the pony. If this is 'made to measure' tack and in good condition then it would be sensible to buy it. If you don't like the look of the tack, or if, for example, the saddle does not fit your rider, then don't be pressured into taking it. Good quality well-fitting tack is the order of the day and if that means splashing out on new (or good second-hand) saddlery then you will just have to do it.

The most important factor in buying your pony is that YOU like him! You are going to have to live with this pony, and even the top champions do not always win. We love our ponies for who they are, not because they win rosettes. So many people think they can 'buy' rosettes and then end up disgruntled when they believe they have wasted their money. This is when tempers flare in the collecting ring. If you love your pony whatever, there is always another day. It goes almost without saying that small children's ponies should always be of a kind temperament, one which allows the child to handle the pony himself. If you buy a pony who has traits which are problems for you, then you will never really be happy with him. At the end of the day, he is going to be a big part of your life, so take your time and make the right decision.

CHAPTER THREE

Conformation

IT IS vitally important that your pony has good conformation and free, straight action. Apart from in style and performance classes, conformation is the second most important mark after jumping. Whilst native ponies need to be a good example of their breed and may need to have certain characteristics relative to that, the basic rules for conformation are the same for any equine.

WHAT TO LOOK FOR

According to one famous judge, 'A working hunter pony should have a good leg at each corner', and this is certainly a good starting point. When you stand back and look at the pony, there should be nothing which stands out as a glaring fault; at first glance everything should appear to be in the right place and in the right proportions. The overall picture should be pleasing with the back neither too short nor too long. The weight of the horse should be evenly distributed, although some emphasis on the quarters provides a better ride. If a pony has a short neck and front, he will make a child sit very near to the front end and therefore be more liable to fall off if the pony makes a mistake. The feeling of having 'nothing in front of you' is one that makes any rider nervous. However, if there is too much neck and head the weight will be concentrated on the forehand making the pony heavy in the hand.

A very narrow pony can make it hard for the rider to get her leg on properly; this may also be a sign of weakness. Similarly a very wide pony will be difficult to sit on and may give a 'rolling ride' which could make a child feel unsafe. Wide ponies can also be difficult to fit with a saddle which will stay in place.

The head should be sensible and attractive, properly set on so as to allow the correct flexion at the throat. There is considerable interest in recent work which shows that the character of a horse can be determined by facial characteristics. A pony with a large, bold eye always looks more friendly and amenable, and this seems to be borne out by the research. Small eyes may denote stubbornness and will also make the head look bigger and less refined. Small ears look neater but large ears should not deter you from buying a pony. They are often a sign of kindness.

Look carefully at the mouth for signs of bitting problems. The teeth should meet evenly and not show signs of excessive wear in any area. Wear of the front teeth almost certainly indicates a crib-biter. Overlapping teeth will mean constant attention from the equine dentist, because the teeth will not wear down normally through eating. A big tongue can produce bitting difficulties and constant dribbling. If you have to constantly wipe your horse's mouth, he will never look quite tidy. Most hunter ponies will eventually go in a double bridle, so there must be room in the mouth for the bits.

The neck should be long enough to give a good length of rein and be set on at a good angle to the shoulder, so that the head is naturally not carried too high or too low. Fat in the throat area will make flexion difficult and cause the head to be carried too high. A weedy neck can be corrected by proper exercise and feeding, but do look carefully to ensure that it is not set on badly, which may also give the impression of lack of neck. The head and neck and the way that they are carried can influence the amount of presence which a horse appears to have. The length of neck should be sufficient for the rider to have something to 'sit behind' but not so much that she feels she is riding by remote control. A scruffy mane is not a problem, unless it has been caused by sweet itch. If you have any suspicions, check the skin in amongst the hairs of the mane. It will remain 'thickened' even when the horse is not rubbing.

The shoulder should slope from the withers to the front of the chest, where it meets the humerus, which in turn should be more or less upright between the shoulder bone (scapula) and the forearm. If the shoulder is too straight it will lead to a head carriage which is too high. A long, flat shoulder and well-defined withers are desirable.

The elbow should have enough room between it and the ribs

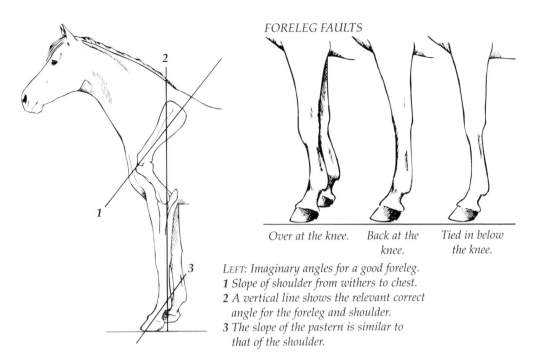

FORELEG FAULTS

Over at the knee.   Back at the knee.   Tied in below the knee.

LEFT: *Imaginary angles for a good foreleg.*
1 *Slope of shoulder from withers to chest.*
2 *A vertical line shows the relevant correct angle for the foreleg and shoulder.*
3 *The slope of the pastern is similar to that of the shoulder.*

to allow freedom of movement. A good shoulder will ensure that movement can be free and straight. The measurement from the withers to the point of the elbow should be similar to that of the distance between the elbow and the ground.

The forelimbs should be set on squarely, without turning in or out at the foot. There should not be too much space between them, which is often a precursor to dishing, nor should they 'come out of the same hole'. Legs which are not symmetrical or straight would generally be considered to have a weakness – something to be avoided in a performance pony. In an older working hunter pony, any sign of puffiness around the joints is often a sign of wear and tear and could contribute to future problems. A reasonably big flat knee, which is bent neither forward or backwards, is ideal. Sometimes the cannon bone below the knee appears to be narrower than it is further down the leg. Such a condition is described as 'tied in below the knee' and can cause tendon problems.

The cannon bone lies between the fetlock and the knee, and at the back of this is a tiny bone called the splint bone. This is sometimes the site of small bony lumps, which usually appear on young ponies who do too much work too soon. They can also occur on slightly older ponies, when perhaps the ground is exceptionally hard. When forming, they may produce heat and swelling and can cause temporary lameness. If a splint is right underneath the knee, it can cause interference to the movement of this joint. Generally, after splints have formed and hardened, they do not give any further trouble. However, they may be seen as a detriment by some judges, usually more in show hunter classes than in workers. If you are buying a pony with splints you will need to bear this in mind.

The feet should be well shaped and in matched pairs. Cracked and brittle feet may be difficult to keep shoes on. Odd-shaped feet may mean a poor farrier or they may indicate a problem – maybe in action. The pastern is a useful guide to the kind of ride you might expect. A short, upright pastern will give a choppy ride. However, a long pastern is a weakness and may cause problems in hard work. A well-proportioned pastern of a sensible length is always best.

Beware of a pony who appears to be wearing unusual shoes. They may be hiding something. For example, a bar shoe may well be fitted to a pony with laminitis. In some cases this can make him go sound, whereas he would not be if the shoe were removed. A pony without any shoes on may be difficult to shoe, or he may just not need them, especially if he is a native. You will obviously have to discuss this with the vendor. Many of the smaller ponies do work very well without shoes, and I had a Welsh Section C who never wore shoes in the winter but was still ridden regularly. Not wearing shoes saves money – and means less damage to little children's toes!

A short, strong **back** is useful for a jumper, but he should have enough rib space for his lungs to work well. Dipped or weak backs will lose conformation marks. A long back will make it difficult to collect the horse up together and is seen as a weakness. It can also be difficult to place the saddle correctly. If the spine behind the saddle is too prominent it may well indicate weak loins. A round, well-muscled rump looks good on a

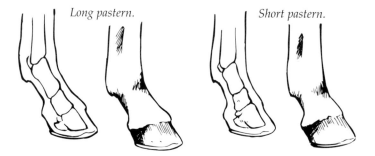

Long pastern. *Short pastern.*

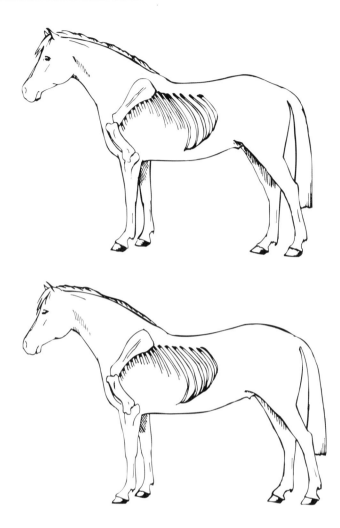

A short, strong back is useful for a jumper.

A long back is seen as a weakness.

hunter pony, although it is thought that a sloping croup aids jumping ability.

The tail should be carried well and should swing gently from side to side when being ridden. If the tail does not move or is even clamped down, it is usually an indication of back problems. The tail, after all, is an extension of the spine.

The hind leg is very important to any performance animal. Ideally, your pony's hind legs should be set on squarely, turning neither in nor out at the hock. The stifle joint should turn very slightly outward to ensure free movement, but not so much as to make the hind movement too wide. When you look at a hind leg, it should be strong and well muscled, and when viewed from the side should appear to have an imaginary straight line running from the point of the buttocks down to the heel. The

HIND LEG FAULTS

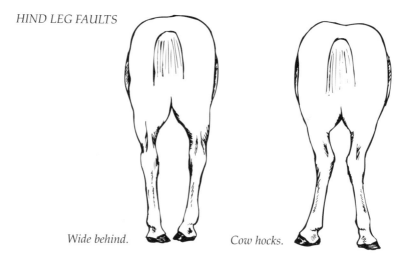

Wide behind.   *Cow hocks.*

muscles on the inside of the thighs should be well developed and when viewed from directly behind should be seen to almost touch. The pasterns should be at the same angle as the feet and neither too short nor too long, which shows weakness.

MOVEMENT

Movement should be straight and free and correct for the breed.

Good movement is one thing that can really catch a judge's eye. Imagine a judge standing in the middle of a big ring at one of the major championships and watching twenty ponies, all of whom have had clear rounds, trotting round at a distance of about thirty yards. Any minor faults which he or she may notice on later, closer inspection will not be visible. Only the outline of the pony, the way it is going and its movement, will really show up. A good, strong, flashy movement will always catch the eye. However, if this movement is not straight, when the pony trots up in hand, it will move him down the line. So you need both straightness when viewed from front and behind and a good strong action when viewed from the side. A worker will be able to get away with a bit more knee lift than a show hunter pony. The latter should have a lower action with more 'toe point', but not the type of movement which appears to come from the fetlocks. The movement should come from the shoulder and well away in front (i.e. the stride should be long and powerful), and it should be well flexed and strong behind.

It is important when assessing conformation to see the horse

Lizzie Winslip and Smoketree Texas Tart, a working hunter pony showing good, strong, straight action.

A beautiful show hunter pony trot from C. Dujardin and Oakley Funny Feeling.

trotted in hand, preferably on a hard surface. The legs should move in a straight line, so much so that when viewed directly from in front, the hind legs are hardly visible behind the front ones. The foot should be placed squarely and evenly on the ground, without twisting in any way. The leg should not swing outwards (dishing) or inwards (plaiting). Sometimes, though, when these faults are found in young horses they can be put down to immaturity and weakness. Each leg of a pair should be just that – matched in length of stride and in the detail of the action. Freedom of movement is very important, so any apparent restriction should be looked at carefully. It may be the first sign of future problems.

Although much can be done to improve the paces, through schooling, it is still important to start with good basics. The walk should be free and swinging with a good long stride. A pony with a good walk will often catch the judge's eye during the final walk-round and may well move up the line for this reason alone. In a good walk, the hind foot should step in front of the print made by the corresponding front foot. The pony should have a good, lively, springy trot with plenty of movement right through the shoulder and plenty of strength in the hind leg. A very common problem with show ponies seems to be what I call the 'drawling' canter – the pony dribbles along the ground with not much life or impulsion. The correct canter should include a moment of suspension and should appear full of impulsion whilst remaining well balanced. The gallop is the ground-covering pace. Far too many show gallops are more closely related to an extended canter than anything else. The ability to really gallop on will always please a hunter judge.

Two examples of faulty movement: in brushing, one leg brushes against the other as the pony moves; in dishing, the front foot is thrown outwards.

Brushing.   *Dishing.*

FIT, OR FAT?

An impression of athleticism is desirable in a working hunter pony. The judge should be able to see that the pony has enough agility to get out of trouble in a difficult situation on the hunting field. If the pony is too fat, it may be that he is kept this way to disguise conformational faults. If he is too thin, you will at least have an opportunity to see his 'frame' and imagine how he will look in show condition. If there is any area which appears to be lacking in muscle development – particularly if this is on one side and not the other – this will need closer inspection.

MOUNTAIN AND MOORLANDS

If you are buying a mountain and moorland pony, you will need to ensure that your chosen pony is a good example of his breed, apart from having all the qualities mentioned above. There are various rules for the different breeds and if you are unsure of these you will need to consult an expert (or a good book!). Most native judges will know these characteristics and will mark down a pony with faults. You should also consider the fact that if he has good conformation and type, he will also be able to compete in the highly competitive ridden classes. If he only jumps – that is all he will do, with any hope of success.

COAT COLOUR

Colour can help in creating a good overall impression and in attracting notice. A bronzed and shiny chestnut or a gleaming bay tend to catch the eye. White socks are another eye-catching asset, as long as they are more or less even. However, too much white on the face (unless it's a grey pony!) can detract from an otherwise smart impression. There are very few coloured ponies competing in hunter classes, possibly because people seem to associate them with a more common type of animal, but there is no reason why a coloured pony, as long as everything else is right about him, should not do very well indeed, especially in worker classes.

Native ponies must be within the colours allowed by their breed society, but again, a good colour is always an advantage.

STAR QUALITY

There is an important quality which should be mentioned here, but which is almost impossible to put into words – it is that of 'presence'. A pony with presence comes into the ring knowing that he is special and that everyone will be looking at him. He goes round with his ears pricked and wearing 'a smile on his face'. He does not look sour nor have his ears back. He holds himself naturally well – in a good shape, but relaxed. You just *have* to notice him. This quality cannot be taught – it will just come naturally to him. However, it can be encouraged by keeping him happy in his work, giving him lots of variety and plenty of playtime in the field, but you will still have to look for it when you first buy him. And you will know it when you see it!.

CHAPTER FOUR

Basic Training

FLATWORK

Whilst too much schooling is not good for any pony and you are (presumably) not aiming to train a Grand Prix dressage horse, some serious flatwork never came amiss. You should either use a manege or a flat, quiet corner of a field.

Children need to be taught from a very early stage to sit deep in the saddle and not lean forward (which is a common fault). When in the correct position, it should be possible to draw an imaginary line from the shoulder, through the hip and down the back of the heel, when viewed from the side. Any deviation from a good riding position will spoil the appearance of the whole picture of pony and rider and reduce the rider's effectiveness in the saddle.

It is vital that your pony learns at the very beginning to stand still whilst being mounted. If your rider has shown him in hand and then has difficulty getting back on board, it is bound to be noticed by the judge. Bad manners will never earn you any extra marks.

Insist that your pony stands still every single time you mount. If he fidgets, dismount immediately. Settle him, and try again. If necessary have an unmounted handler at the pony's head, and make sure the pony is praised when he stands still.

Next go on to the walk. Remember that in your ridden show, when all the ponies have gone round together, you will be called back to walk and this is when the judge starts arranging the class in some sort of order. A bold, swinging walk will always catch the eye. Far too many competitors come down from canter with a few dishevelled trotting strides then practically collapse into a shambling walk. When the judge is looking at

Dressed for schooling at home. Notice the boots on the pony's legs.

you, this is just not good enough. The pony should be kept in a steady rhythm with his hocks engaged in any downward transition. If he is too much on the forehand, he will give the impression of pulling himself along with the front end rather than driving from behind. A really good swinging walk, without hurrying, can be cultivated whilst out hacking. Purposeful is the word which springs to mind to describe the best walking action.

Moving off from halt is also important. The pony should go forward at the slightest pressure of the rider's leg. This is particularly important at that moment when you have stood in front of the judge and he or she asks you to move off and perform your show. If your pony has problems with this, you will have to use a long stick at home and back up the leg aid with a sharp smack with the stick, applied as far back on the quarters as you can reach. The pony will soon get into the habit of moving off smartly and you can dispense with the stick.

The **walk** is a four-time pace, with the hind feet touching the ground in front of the print of the fore feet, but when walking in a straight line, the prints should be in two evenly spaced straight tracks. A word here about head carriage. Whatever pace your pony is in, a good head carriage will always enhance his appearance. Too high, and the pony will look 'hot'; too low, and he will look 'dopey'. Overbending makes him look strong, and 'poking his nose' out looks very sloppy. In the case of an overly high head carriage, the rider should maintain a steady contact and then ask the pony to lower his head with a gentle squeezing action on the reins, using a give-and-take action whilst keeping a contact with the legs. If the head is too low, the rider must push it up with a good strong leg aid, whilst keeping contact on the reins to control the pace.

The **trot** has a different rhythm, being a two-time pace. It should be balanced and active. The horse should move on alternate diagonal pairs of legs and exhibit a short period of suspension in between. A good exercise in trot is to shorten the stride on the short sides of the school and lengthen it on the long sides. This will improve control and allow the rider to lengthen the trot in front of the judge, in the ring, and thus show off the pony to his best advantage. Practise doing this without substantially altering your speed, so that the pony is more athletic and powerful looking. Trotting up and down hills is another good exercise, which helps in balancing the pony and building hindquarter muscles.

If you intend to compete in style and performance classes (and even if you don't), trot serpentines are a good way of improving balance. By changing direction and bend, the pony's suppleness should improve. A serpentine usually has three loops of as near to equal size as you can achieve. There should be two or three strides in which the pony goes completely straight before going off on the other bend. The rider will also have an opportunity to change diagonal (if a rider does not know which is the correct diagonal, the thing to remember is to sit when the outside shoulder comes back towards you – which is when you put your leg on in rising trot). Although you might see dressage riders doing sitting trot when doing serpentines, young riders and inexperienced ponies should always practise this exercise in rising trot.

Canter is a three-time pace. Cantering on the correct leg is obviously something to practise, as you will want to get this right in the ring. Any cantering at a show must be relaxed and sensible. Rushing round, overtaking others and so on, looks dreadful. It is important for the rider to remember to use both legs, together with the seat and back, to establish a good canter. At home, practise cantering along bridlepaths or round your fields in a steady, even pace.

The best way to establish a nice rhythmical canter is to ride on a twenty-metre circle. The pony must work around the rider's inside leg, neither collapsing into the centre nor swinging his quarters out. It is an interesting exercise to mark out a completely round circle in your schooling area and then see how close to this you actually go. Children, in particular, are very good at 'oval' circles.

For a canter serpentine, bring the pony back to trot for a stride or two in between the loops, before you strike off on the other lead. Flying changes are only expected from experts.

The **gallop** is the favourite pace of most ponies. A showing

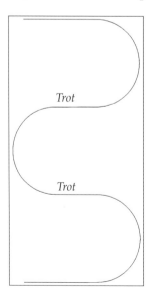

A canter serpentine. To get the correct leg for the canter, trot a few straight strides to change the rein, as you cross the centre line.

gallop needs only to be performed along one long side of the ring, and the transitions up and down must be very clear. The best way to practise this is to gallop on for a few strides when cantering round the school. Do not allow the pony to 'take off', just encourage him to lengthen his stride and lower his head and neck slightly, then immediately bring him back to canter and settle him in a rhythm before repeating the exercise. If he is reluctant to gallop on in the ring, tuck him in behind someone who looks lively and go with them. If he is likely to get over-excited, make sure that you have a big space in front of you – and then let him just go on naturally rather than sending him on.

A square halt, in front of the judge, is most important. In early training, it is quite difficult for a pony to do a proper square halt, with his hocks engaged, and he is therefore better just to do a still halt. If the rider agitates the horse, in an effort to get him absolutely square, it may result in a fidgeting pony. The pony should gradually be ridden up into his bridle more when halting, so that his weight is evenly distributed on all four legs. Any sign of fidgeting should be corrected by going back a few stages in training.

IN-HAND TRAINING

Whilst perfecting your ridden flatwork, it is also important to practise standing up your pony and running him up in hand. This is especially vital for a young or inexperienced pony who has not been shown in hand. Stewards are never very thrilled about having to chase a pony, flapping their score sheets to try and get it to trot. If you are starting with a young pony – perhaps one you have bought with an eye to the future – do show him in a few hunter pony in-hand classes. These provide good practice, and when you get to run him up in-hand at your first ridden competition, there should be no problem.

It is also important to practise standing him up in hand. By doing this correctly, you show him off to his best advantage. He should be square in front but the hind leg nearest to the judge should be very slightly behind the other one. If the judge moves round to the other side, ask your pony to change the position of his back legs accordingly. The head should be held in a natural position. Holding it up in the air is only for Welsh Cob stallions and the like. Don't teach this exercise with tit-bits or your pony may learn to bite you – or worse still the judge – in the ring. Just praise him when he is right and put him into the correct position when he is not. Most ponies learn these things really quickly. The business of throwing handfuls of grass in the air to attract his attention and/or get his head up, is no substitute for practice at home. One useful device that we have employed is to hold the rider's stick or cane on the end of the pony's muzzle. This concentrates his attention and he soon learns that it means he has to stand up and stand still.

OVERBENDING

The biggest single ridden problem with working hunter ponies (and sometimes show hunters) is overbending. This is an evasion – and it looks dreadful. The following sequence of events is typical – after a worker has been in the ring and jumped, he then goes back in the ring (where the jumps are), this time with several other ponies; his little rider hangs on for dear life as the pony gets faster and faster and eventually embeds his

Aston True Welshman, in his first outing in a double bridle, shows a classic case of overbending.

head in his chest and goes for it. One exercise that can be taught to children and that can help is the **half-halt.** The rider must first put the leg on and squeeze the rein to get the pony's attention. This puts the weight back into the hindquarters, thus lightening the front end and bringing the head up again. The rider should then immediately release the rein pressure. The whole exercise should only take a second or two and is designed to bring the pony under better control. When children are first learning this, they are sometimes reluctant to apply the leg aid (accelerate), preferring instead to hang onto the reins (brake) – but this exercise does work with all but the most determined puller and done correctly will make your pony a better ride.

MAKING THE MOST OF HACKING

Variety is the spice of life and some of the transitions and other movements that you will need in the ring can be practised whilst out hacking or in other situations. For example, when deciding to trot on a hack, ride as if you were trotting on in front of the judge and do the same when you come back down to walk. Ensure that you have the correct bend when going round a corner, i.e. that the pony's head is turned slightly towards the direction of movement and the neck is nicely bent. If you are cantering on, say up a bridlepath (you should never canter on the road or a grass verge), practise riding a controlled canter, and if there is an opportunity, gallop on for ten strides and then come back to canter. These kinds of exercise are all part of a good education yet without seeming like schooling.

A word of warning about hacking on the roads. Your pony should never go out without adequate leg protection. Always put on knee boots and schooling boots. A fall on the road will inevitably result in scarring if there is no protection.

MORE ADVANCED SUPPLING EXERCISES

Suppling exercises such as shoulder-in and half-pass are very useful for any pony, but particularly for one who is going on to jump. They should only be carried out by a reasonably experienced rider as a novice can do more harm than good. Ask your instructor to help you with these.

MANNERS

Manners are a very important part of any pony's training. Whilst things such as standing still whilst being mounted will have been taught at home, there are others which make life much easier which he will only learn by experience. These are things such as standing in a crowd of strangers in the collecting ring, without kicking or biting other ponies; standing still whilst hoof oil is put on or girths tightened; waiting his turn at the practice jump without getting excited, and so on. If you insist that your pony behaves properly from the very beginning, he will grow up with good habits. If you once let him misbehave – say, by biting his neighbour in the line-up, for example – he will do it again and again and end up being a perfect pest. This does not mean that you should beat him up in the ring if he does wrong. In a class you will just have to cover up his bad behaviour as best you can and then make sure you are firm with him at home. Taking him to the lorry and thrashing him will not work either – he will not know what he has done by then and you will attract adverse attention to yourself (and rightly).

CHAPTER FIVE

Jumping

THIS IS the most important part of the whole working hunter pony competition. If your pony does not jump a clear round (or at worst collect minimal faults) then you are wasting your time. If you are inexperienced there is no substitute for lessons with a professional trainer. A good instructor will be able to put your rider into a good position to negotiate fences safely and effectively, and teach your pony to tackle his fences with confidence. However, if you intend to undertake some of the training yourself or you need to improve your performance then read on!

THE YOUNG PONY

The final aim for your young pony is to make him a bold, confident jumper who takes a course of fences safely, without rushing or needing to be coaxed round. He must not spook or refuse, and these are problems which arise during training. To help instill confidence, the unbroken pony can be shown in hand; he should also be led about around the stables or in quiet lanes to further his education. He should be gradually introduced to a range of 'strange' sights and sounds, such as shavings being shaken out of a plastic sack in his stable, rugs hanging over doors and similar sights. If he is particularly nervous you can hang plastic bottles on (secure) rope, or lengths of cloth or sacking, in his stable; this way he will soon get used to things hanging and flapping, so that when he sees a fluttering banner in a show ring, it will not distract his attention from the job in hand.

Presuming that you have backed your pony and are riding

him, and that he is at least four years old, you should start taking him to shows and events and just ride him around the showground. Let him see all the spooky and noisy things that go on. Reassure him that you are there and that he WILL be safe, and he will soon gain confidence.

EARLY JUMPING LESSONS

At this stage, if you have the facilities, loose schooling over a couple of low, uncomplicated jumps can help him to find his balance and get the feel of jumping without having to bother about the weight of the rider. Apart from a headcollar (which will enable you to catch him) he should not be wearing any tack – which might get caught up in the jump stands or whatever – but he should have adequate leg protection. If he doesn't seem to know what to do, encourage him to participate with a lungeing whip. Often, ponies find loose jumping great fun and, once they've got the hang of it, can be turned into the manege to 'jump themselves'.

Lungeing over jumps can be a bit tricky, especially if you have tall jump stands. You can, instead, lunge over trotting poles on the ground or small jumps without wings, if you really want to. Personally, I prefer to start ponies off by free jumping them first then going straight on to jumping under saddle. As a pony will be expected to jump with the weight of a rider on his back, he may as well learn to balance himself in these circumstances as soon as possible.

Early jumping with a rider should always be done in a simple snaffle bridle. A running martingale will stop him throwing his head up too high and provide the rider with a neck strap. You should always use schooling boots. A knock on the leg will destroy confidence in some ponies.

Introduce jumping by bringing in trotting poles in your schooling work and by letting him trot over fallen branches and small ditches when out hacking. If he has an experienced companion to follow, it will help his confidence. If your pony is apprehensive about trotting poles, start by walking him over a single pole and gradually build up to a maximum of six. The distances should be set according to the size of the pony and the length of his stride. The most important factor at this stage is not to frighten him or put him off in any way. During this early phase, be prepared for a big ungainly jump at any time – even when previous jumps have been smooth. Always have a neck strap to hold on to.

When your pony is confidently trotting over poles on the ground, you can put up a small cross-pole. It helps either to have wings to guide him towards the fence, or to erect the fence against one side of the school or field. Keep in trot until he can jump several, well-spaced small cross-poles (at least five strides apart). Always approach in a straight line, never using sharp turns. You will probably find that one day, your pony naturally takes a few strides of canter in front of the fence, but never rush him into this. Mistakes made now will probably show for the rest of his life. Most faults are caused by fear instilled during early training.

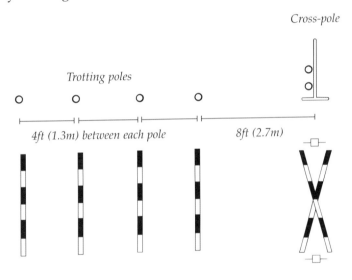

Cross-pole

Trotting poles

4ft (1.3m) between each pole

8ft (2.7m)

A simple first grid.

Now is the time to introduce different fences, such as a straight pole (with a ground pole) or a small spread. Spread fences are important for the working hunter pony as they teach him to jump with a hunting style rather than the more 'upright' way of going of a show-jumping pony. Do not overface him or frighten him by using strange fillers – this comes later. He should also learn about doubles, making sure that the spacing is correct (approximately 35ft/10.5m for a double with two strides in the middle).

Cavalletti and trotting poles in various combinations have several important values. They help to develop balance and style and allow the pony to develop a rhythm and good stride. A

Increase the complexity by adding a spread fence to the simple trotting grid.

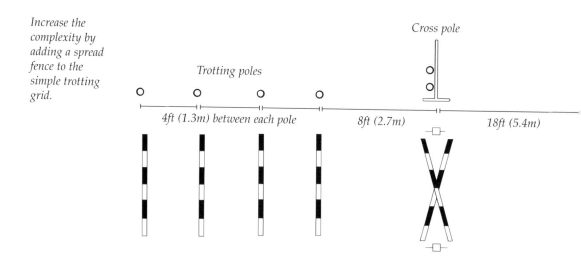

mixture of poles and small fences give him plenty to think about, thus keeping him calmer and more focused on what he is doing.

PRACTISING AT HOME

If you want to build a course to jump at home and are setting up doubles and combinations, start with the distances suggested in the schooling exercises and adjust them according to your pony's stride.

It is not necessary to have fancy, ready-made jumps to practise over – although of course it is very nice if you can afford them. You can make your own jumps fairly easily with a bit of ingenuity. Concentrate on the types of fence you are likely

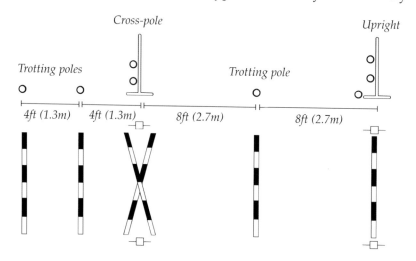

Small trotting grid for average 13hh pony.

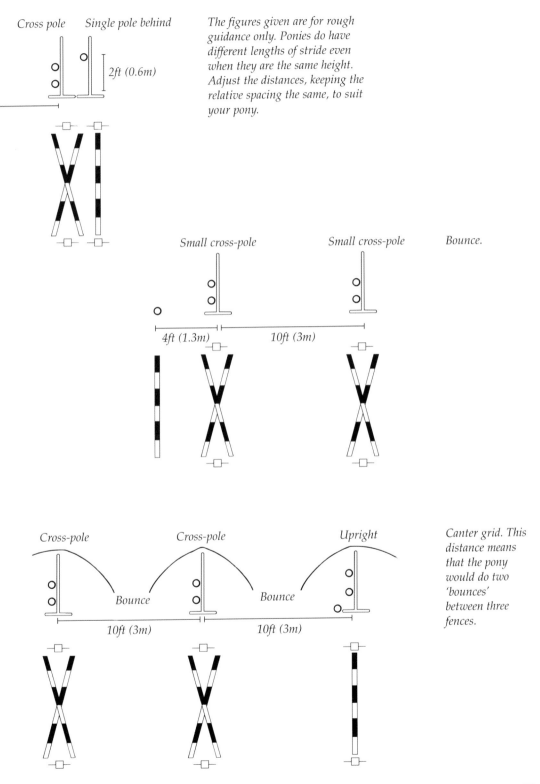

Cross pole   Single pole behind

2ft (0.6m)

The figures given are for rough guidance only. Ponies do have different lengths of stride even when they are the same height. Adjust the distances, keeping the relative spacing the same, to suit your pony.

Small cross-pole   Small cross-pole   Bounce.

4ft (1.3m)   10ft (3m)

Cross-pole   Cross-pole   Upright   Canter grid. This distance means that the pony would do two 'bounces' between three fences.

Bounce   Bounce

10ft (3m)   10ft (3m)

to meet in competition. As long as you use safe and sturdy materials you can easily create lots of different courses, purely by moving your materials around regularly.

- Fillers and walls – you can make a good solid pair of fillers by cutting a wooden pallet in half. Do remember to knock in or remove any protruding nails.

- Jump stands can be improvised from plastic barrels or milk crates, or you could treat yourself to some plastic jump blocks specifically designed for the purpose.

- Poles – round fencing rails, available quite cheaply from timber merchants, make good poles. These rails can also be cut into smaller sections to build a stile (see below).

- Bullfinches and other brush fences are common. Start with a few twigs in the top of a fence and gradually build up to a more bushy appearance.

- Water, either in trays or in a small ditch, can be simulated by buying a couple of cheap plastic cat-litter trays and filling them with water. Start by jumping them empty. The rider should not look down at the water, but look ahead and give the pony confidence.

- Stiles are nearly always a feature. Gradually make a fence narrower until you get it to about 6ft/1.8m wide, which would be the minimum for a stile. Use two poles leaning on each end of the fence and running out to the front each side as guidelines to keep your pony straight, rather than let him run out.

Use poles to guide the pony towards a narrow fence. A box or other object can be used as a 'step' in the middle of an improvised stile.

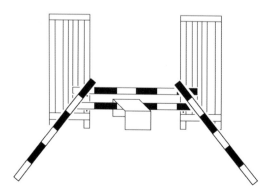

BUILDING CONFIDENCE

Around this time you should be thinking of tackling a clear round competition, which you will find at most small shows. Let the pony take his time and keep calm. Take a long track with wide circles and straight approaches, and try to keep in a steady rhythm.

Everything you do at this stage should be aimed at building confidence. Hunting is a very good education for a young horse. He will learn to pop over natural obstacles and to balance himself on different going. The unfamiliar countryside and the accompanying sights and sounds are all important experiences. Do not, however, get carried away and overtire a young pony. This will quickly sour him.

Pony Club activities are wonderful for children. Rallies are often held at local riding establishments with good facilities and children and ponies can learn a great deal from experienced riders, and at very little cost.

Competing in show hunter classes can be a useful exercise, even if your pony is destined to be a worker; and cross-country and hunter trials can help to increase confidence in both horse and rider. Nowadays, there are a number of cross-country

Hunting is a good education for a young horse and is always good to 'sharpen up' a lazy pony.

courses which are open to the public for schooling rounds. Look out for one and take your pony round it. Leave out any obstacles which are too high or too wide for his stage of training. It is better not to attempt a fence than have several refusals and then have to give up on it.

Never over-jump a young pony. Jumping lessons must be interspersed with hacking, hunting, schooling on the flat and so on. Variety really is important when it comes to training horses and your aim is to present him in the ring for his first real competition in a confident and happy frame of mind.

A word here about the ground that you are riding on. Slippery ground can quickly spoil confidence, although studs can help. Ponies should always be allowed time to get used to studs before they are used in competition. We always used to fit just one stud in the outside corner of the shoe, but current veterinary thinking believes that this unbalances the foot and may cause leg problems. It is now recommended that two studs are fitted, one at each end of the shoe. If the ground is too hard, a young pony may jar his legs or even injure himself and this may put him off. An older pony will compensate by using less effort, taking short strides and barely skimming the top of the fence. This could cause knocked-down poles.

COMMON JUMPING FAULTS

Rushing

This can either be caused by training or riding faults. If during training the pony starts to get excited and rush into his fences, he should be taken away from the fence to do something else for a while. When attempting to jump again, it may help to do so on a circle, thus limiting the forward impulsion. If you try to hold the pony back, it will only increase the problem by building up his frustration.

Sometimes ponies rush because of a previous experience of pain. If he has been jabbed in the mouth or pinched by badly fitting saddlery, you should find out exactly what the problem is, rectify it, and then go back several stages in his training and rebuild his confidence. If you cannot find the problem yourself, you must seek professional advice. Such problems as back pain or other pains cannot readily be diagnosed by the amateur, but can be the cause of all sorts of jumping problems.

The pony who rushes off after the fence should be brought back to jumping from trot to curb this habit. There could, however, be a physical cause for this, such as leg pain which is brought on by landing, so this should be properly investigated.

Napping and refusing

These problems are often the result of an intelligent pony taking advantage of his small rider's inexperience; this kind of naughtiness is particularly found in small ponies. Poor initial training and/or bad riding by previous riders allow these habits to become ingrained, and as a consequence they are very difficult to eradicate. It may help to go back to early training and not to return to the later stages until all is going well. Riders can gain confidence and experience by riding an older schoolmaster and then returning to their own pony. Napping and/or refusing can also be caused by pain, in the legs, mouth or back or from ill-fitting saddlery. Fear arising from a bad experience or inexperience is another cause, as is poor or slippery going or overfacing. Very few ponies are actually downright disobedient, and unless the cause is absolutely clear, professional advice should always be sought. The advent of the video camera has provided riders and trainers with a very useful problem-solving tool.

Lack of fitness

This can manifest in refusing or in running out or just general laziness. Poles knocked off are another sign, as is a lack of scope. A tired pony can show a temporary reluctance to jump. If your pony is blowing a lot after working, or sweating excessively, then he may well not be fit enough for the job in hand. Work on his fitness before you ask him to jump again.

JUMPING IN THE RING

Before you take your pony into the ring to jump, he must be sufficiently warmed up on the flat. This ensures that his muscles are relaxed and working, that he has settled down in his surroundings and that he is listening to the rider. Every horse varies in the amount of work he needs before a competition and you will have to learn this by trial and error. As soon as you feel that he is ready, you can attempt one or two practice jumps. A plain pole will do. If you have done your homework properly, you should not need to construct huge fences draped with branches and horse blankets and whatever. The collecting ring is not the place for learning – it is too late then.

Before warming up, you should walk the course on foot, using the line that you will take when you are on the pony. Look at doubles and combinations and check the striding. You will quickly learn to assess a combination just by looking at it – instinctively you will know how many strides there should be between each fence.

Do not think too much about any fence that you perceive as difficult or spooky – just ride it like any other. If you look ahead and expect your pony to get you safely to the other side, he probably will. This is not contradictory to the advice given above for schooling over cross-country fences. All the fences which appear in a worker class in the ring will be made to a pre-scribed height and width and therefore the ponies in that class should be capable of taking them on. On a cross-country course, schooling fences are usually set up in a variety of heights and widths to suit different competitors, so you would not be expected to jump them all.

Rider nerves are easily picked up by ponies, who think to themselves, 'So you don't like this fence then? Well let's not bother to jump it.' Go into the class with an optimistic attitude – and above all enjoy yourself!

CHAPTER SIX

Grooming and Turn-out

GROOMING

Grooming is a very important part of any horse's routine. Apart from the obvious removal of dirt, grooming stimulates circulation and massages the muscles. In the wild, a pony would roll much more than he has the time to do when he is only in a field for a limited time. He would also rub himself on low branches, particularly if he had a sore or aching place.

Ponies naturally have a longer and more oily coat in winter, to protect them from the weather, so the winter grooming regime is necessarily different to the summer one, when the coat is short and sleek. The winter regime for a clipped pony is similar to that for summer care, except that you should compensate for his missing coat by putting rugs on and, when grooming, just uncover part of him at a time.

Keep your grooming kit clean and tidy, and in one place. Dirty brushes merely transfer dirt back onto the pony – and may spread germs and fungal infections such as ringworm. For day-to-day care the normal contents of a grooming kit could be:

• dandy brush – for mud removal and use on long winter coats

• plastic or rubber curry comb – can be used directly on very dirty or moulting ponies and also to clean the body brush

• comb – for plaiting, pulling manes and tails, and combing through mane and tail before showing

• cloths and sponges – for washing off marks, cleaning nose and eyes etc., and final polishing (NB: keep a separate sponge for dock and sheath area and for each pony)

• hoof pick

• hoof oil and brush

In winter, it will be very difficult to show an unclipped pony in winter championship classes. His coat will be too thick to groom with any degree of success. Indeed you would not want to remove all the natural oils which are part of the pony's protection against wind and rain. A dandy brush and/or plastic curry comb can be used to remove mud and dirt, but there is not much else you can do. The feet should be picked out regularly and the condition of the feet and/or shoes monitored.

The summer coat is much easier to care for, as is a clipped or partly clipped pony. Regular body brushing will keep dirt to a minimum, whilst toning up the circulation.

Gentle massaging of muscular areas is much enjoyed and helps to remove any slight stiffness which working may have caused. Check the whole body surface when grooming for minor injuries and possible areas of heat. This may avoid a small problem escalating.

Wisping or banging is a useful procedure for an animal with a poor neck or quarters. If you are very clever, you can make a wisp from hay (there are full instructions in The British Horse Society *Manual of Horsemanship*) or you can buy a ready made leather pad or use a folded towel. Wisping activates the oil-producing glands of the skin and brings a shine to the coat as well as improving muscle tone. The action should be to bring the wisp down with a bang, followed by stroking in the direction of the coat. This should be done just hard enough so that the muscle contracts in readiness for the next stroke. At least thirty strokes per day, each side of the neck should show a result in about a month. Wisping should never be done on bony areas or on the tender areas of the loins.

If the mane hangs on the wrong side, it can damped and plaited over during the night – but do not make the plaits too tight or they may cause the pony to rub. This will make the mane easier to plait, or to lie right for mountain and moorland classes. Native ponies with very thick manes and tails can have them brushed with a plastic curry comb which will pull out some of the hairs in a more natural way than pulling. Thin manes and tails should not be brushed at all; instead any straw and debris can be picked out by hand and then the mane and/or tail occasionally washed carefully with a mild shampoo.

There are a number of proprietary coat-gloss products on the market which make grooming, and particularly mane and tail management, much easier. If you brush them through a clean mane and tail, you will find that they leave a residual coating on the hair which repels dirt and also helps to make removal of shavings or other bedding much easier. The effect lasts for several weeks so their use saves time and effort on a daily basis.

If your pony has white socks it is worth keeping them reasonably clean as part of your normal grooming; you will then avoid the problem of finding them very stained when you want to go to a show. However, too much washing should be avoided as this may lead to sore skin or conditions such as mud fever. The best method is to brush the legs when they are dry and then scrub any stained areas with a flannel dipped in hot water and coat conditioner then well wrung out.

If you are going to have to plait the pony's tail or if he needs a pulled tail, it is well worth pulling out a few long hairs whilst you are grooming. This saves having a mammoth pulling session just before a show, which may well upset the pony and make him sore.

A good coat starts with good management and feeding. If you clip a pony who has a dull, staring coat, you will just get a shorter version of the same. Your aim should be to have your pony gleaming with health, even when he is filthy in the field.

BATHING YOUR PONY

Bathing should only really be done in good weather. To make your pony soaking wet in a cold wind is asking for trouble. If you do decide to bath him, get everything ready before you start so that he does not get cold or bored. You will need: lots of WARM water; either some proprietary horse shampoo or a mild human version from the supermarket (which is much cheaper!); a sweat scraper; towels; a sweat sheet or special drying rug (Thermatex or similar); and chalk or other products (such as coat conditioner) if you have a specific need for them.

Start at the head end and work back, leaving the legs until last – when you can have him rugged up. Native ponies can have

Grey horses will need more frequent washes to keep them clean.

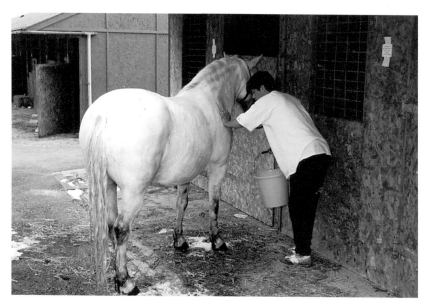

conditioner put on their manes and tails, but if you are plaiting, this will make it difficult to grasp the hair. Rinse thoroughly, as shampoo left in can cause scurf. Scrape off as much water as possible and dry the pony's face and any drips with the towel. Rug him up well quickly, unless you have drying lamps, and if necessary walk him around to get him warm. Then wash his legs, taking care to dry his heels carefully. If he has white socks, they may need to be scrubbed with a proprietary whitener and then have chalk applied whilst the legs are still damp, before being well bandaged.

TIPS FOR GREY PONIES

White greys can be very difficult to clean and to keep clean. Solid bar household soap is good for stains, and for persistent stains, an application of hydrogen peroxide, used as per the instructions on the bottle, can do the trick. White tails can be plaited up and then covered with a tail bandage which secures a stocking or tights leg over the ends. A deep summer sheet tucked under the belly, a hood, and leg bandages from hoof to knee should mean that he is still clean the next morning!

If your pony is stabled at home, it is well worth skipping out just before you go to bed, especially if your pony is usually dirty in the box.

CLIPPING AND TRIMMING

Clipping is carried out to facilitate better drying off after work; to enable the pony to do more work without distress; and to help keep him clean and tidy.

A great deal can be done to improve your pony's shape and appearance with careful thought as to clipping and trimming. For example, you can make a light-boned animal look more substantial by leaving leg hair on but clipping the rest. Conformational faults can be hidden – but can also be made to look worse if you do not think about what you are doing. There is nothing so awful as a pony with a long back wearing a hunter clip with the saddle patch right up his withers, making his back look longer still!

If you are inexperienced at clipping and trimming, ask someone else to do it for you – if you clip anything off by mistake you cannot put it back on. In this respect, do be careful not to clip too near to the mane. It is better to have a slim fringe of unclipped hair along the mane (which in emergencies can be stuck down with gel) than to spend all the next summer trying to grow out the little spiky bits of mane which you cut off by mistake. Make sure that your clippers are sharp and that they do not overheat, which can make the pony fidgety. Cover him up as you go along. If he gets cold, he will move around more and that is when you might make a mistake.

After clipping, the pony will have a layer of greasy dirt on the surface of his coat, even if he looked clean before you started. The best way to deal with this is to exercise him to open the pores and then give him a thorough grooming with a nice soft body brush. A good way to clean a clipped coat but without washing the pony is to use fairly hot water and a rough flannel. Simply wring out the flannel so that is just damp and use it (without any soap) to 'groom' the pony using circular movements. You will be surprised how much dirt this lifts off.

A few weeks after clipping, some ponies grow a layer of longer hairs where they have been clipped; these are known as 'cat hairs'. Old stable management books talk of singeing off cat hairs with a blow torch, but thankfully this practice has died out! If you are careful you can run the clippers lightly over the stragglers, without applying any pressure, and take off just the long top hair, or else you can just wait until you do a second clip and take them off then. It really depends on how scruffy your pony looks if they are left on.

Clipping the top of a tail looks dreadful and is not recommended. A small portion of the mane can be carefully removed for the headpiece of the bridle (but not for natives).

Native ponies can be clipped, if the breed society regulations allow. The heels are never trimmed, and the jaw clipped only very carefully so that it does not show. Ponies who qualify for the Olympia championships (in December) can be clipped right out, with the exception of feather, if it is done early enough. The pony will then grow another, finer coat, especially if he is kept rugged up well.

Types of clip

• **Full clip** – With a full clip the whole of the coat is removed. This can look good on a pony who is somewhat on the stocky side or who has short thick legs. The removal of hair from the legs makes the legs look finer, but care should be taken that mud fever or cracked heels do not develop to spoil his beauty. If you opt for this type of clip, you can coat the legs with Vaseline or other water-repellent substance before you turn him out in wet weather.

• **Hunter clip** – In a hunter clip the body and head are clipped out but hair is left on the legs, and sometimes on a saddle patch as well. Hair on the legs will protect them and can have the effect of making fine limbs look more substantial. It is a real skill to clip a neat saddle patch, although a numnah can be used as a guideline. If you put the saddle patch too far forward or too far back, you will change the appearance of your pony. You can, of course, use this to your advantage, but only attempt it if you have had plenty of practice.

• **Blanket and trace clips** – These come in all sorts of variations, whereby hair is removed in various degrees. Usually the underneath of the belly and the neck are clipped as a minimum, but the other extreme is the true blanket clip, when just the legs and an area corresponding to a quarter sheet is left. The lines of the clip can change the appearance of your pony dramatically – for example, a clip which goes up the neck with a sweeping line, higher in the centre than the ends, will make the neck look fuller.

Clipping should be done around September or October and then a second clip, if necessary, should be done in December. Clipping of the underneath of the jaw and the back of the heels (not for natives) can be done at any time. With practice you should be able to blend any trimming into the surrounding coat, without leaving a tell-tale line.

TRIMMING TIPS

• **Head** – Trimming the underneath of the jaw and getting the hair to blend in smoothly with the longer hairs on the side of the head is not an easy thing at all! You need to hold the hairs out sideways and run the clippers through them in such a way that when you get to the edge of the area you want to clip, you are hardly clipping anything off at all. You need to do the same thing at the point where the head meets the neck.

• **Whiskers and eyelashes** – Whether or not to cut off the whiskers is really a matter of personal choice, although a pony with a big head will always look a little better if you trim off any untidy hair. Eyelashes should never, ever be trimmed; and the practice of using the clippers to remove hair around the eyes to make them look bigger is downright silly. It is difficult enough to clip around the eyes when doing a full clip. You may find that some ponies have problems eating if you cut their whiskers off. This is because ponies use their whiskers as feelers – so it is really kinder to leave them on. As long as the pony is neatly turned out, it will not matter. Owners of natives should never cut their ponies' whiskers off.

• **Legs and heels** – Some ponies, even in their summer coat, have long hairs on the back of their legs – sometimes even if they have no actual feather. If they pull out easily, you can tease out a few each time you groom. If not, you can hold the hair out sideways from the leg and run the clippers up against the lie of the hair growth. If you do not cut closely, this can look very natural, but it must be done properly. The same applies to feather. Starting at the heel, the hair should be held outwards and the clippers moved upwards, gradually allowing more length of hair to be left as you get nearer to the fetlock joint. Sometimes long 'feather' hairs extend up the back of the pastern. In this case just carry on up to an appropriate point and then taper off. Native ponies should never have any feather removed. If you are doing British Show Pony Society and native classes, you will just have to stick the feather down with hair gel!

THE MANE

For British Show Pony Society classes, ponies have to be plaited and therefore the mane, unless it is very short and thin, will need to be pulled.

Pulling a mane

This is best done either on a warm day or just after exercise, when the pores are open. You should remove the longest hairs from underneath, either by winding them round a comb or your fingers. Comb the mane through at regular intervals during pulling so that any long ends will show. If your pony is fidgety or the mane is very thick, you will have to do a whole mane in several sessions.

Never pull the hairs on the top of the mane or attempt to cut off any short hairs in this area with scissors – in fact scissors should never be anywhere near the mane, except to cut the plaiting cotton! Don't pull the mane too short, or you will never get hold of it properly to do your plaits.

Plaiting a mane

Plaits should always be sewn in with cotton which matches the mane. Elastic bands should only be used in a dire emergency and they should never be white – unless your pony has a white mane. It used to be said that there should be an odd number of plaits in the mane, usually seven or nine. Nowadays you can really use any number (although you always use only one for the forelock). Plaits can be employed to good use to enhance the overall effect. A long neck can shortened by fewer and bigger plaits, and vice-versa. A weak neck should always have its plaits put on top of the mane, rather than to one side.

Start by combing the mane thoroughly and then dividing it into equal sections, each secured with a rubber band, to correspond with the eventual plaits. Adjust the 'bunches' if you find

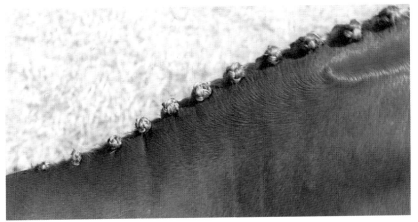

Neat and tidy plaits.

you have more mane at one end than the other or if your bunches look uneven. Then thread your needle and cotton. Use a double length of thread with a knot in the end. It should be about 15in./35cm long. Take your first section and dab on some hair gel or mousse (the kind designed for human use). Divide the hair into three sections and plait *tightly.* Wind the end of your cotton round the end of the plait and then push the needle through between the threads, making a knot. Fold the plait up neatly into a roll and then stitch through the whole plait. If you are dealing with an unruly mane, you may find it helpful to take the cotton discreetly round one side of the base of the plait, through the middle and then round the other so that any short ends are secured. Do not wind the cotton round the base of the plait – this does not look right. Cut off your needle and any remaining thread, close to the plait.

When taking your plaits out be very careful not to cut off chunks of mane – you will have none left by the end of the season.

If you have a very dirty pony, or you need to leave plaits in overnight, the leg of a stocking or pair of tights can be secured over the plaits, using elastic bands. This will help to keep them clean. If leaving plaits in for any length of time, leave the fore-lock and the last one or two plaits in the withers area loose, for the sake of the comfort of the pony.

Tidying a mane

For native classes, you should not really touch the mane at all. However, if you have long straggly ends, you can remove these with an old clipper blade. This will give a more natural look than scissors. Regular washing will avoid a mane getting too dirty and possibly prevent the pony from rubbing it. False manes are not yet available, so bear this in mind!

THE TAIL

British Show Pony Society ponies have a pulled tail or, occasionally, if there is some reason for not pulling, a very neatly plaited tail.

Pulling a tail

To start pulling, comb the tail through very thoroughly. Commence pulling at the top of one side of the tail and right underneath. Pull out just a few hairs at a time, either by winding them round a comb or, if they are very short, by grasping them with pliers. Work down one side of the tail to about half or two thirds of the way down the dock and then do the same on the other side. You may need to spread this process over several sessions. Look carefully at the tail and see that it looks right. If not, pull it a little further down. Gradually work towards the centre, leaving the centre hairs very slightly longer, so that they lie down when bandaged. It helps to run your fingers through each side of the tail, pulling the hairs out to the side, so that you can see which are the longest hairs.

Plaiting a tail

This is a very difficult thing to do and needs lots of practice. The tail will have been left long at the top, so the first thing to do is to comb it out carefully. Some hair gel may help you to grasp the hair more easily and will also seal in short ends. You need to take a small bunch of hair from each side, ensuring that this is the hair at the very edge of the dock. Using these bunches and a third one from the centre of the tail, start a plaiting action. Continue in this manner, drawing in small, equal-sized bunches from alternate sides, always ensuring that you do not miss any hairs. When you get down to the bottom of the dock (or wherever you want your plaiting to end) the remaining hairs in your hand should be made into an ordinary plait. This is then secured

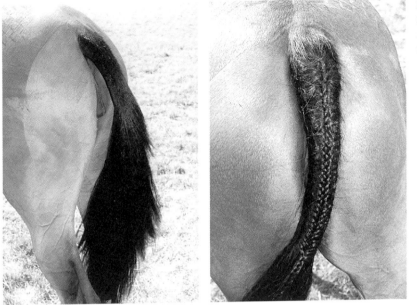

at the end with cotton and sewn back up, just in one loop, to the bottom of the main plait. The whole can then be smoothed over and secured with another coat of gel.

Tidying the tail

The end of the tail is cut off level, approximately half way, or slightly less, between the hock and the ground. The tail should be held in the position that it is carried naturally, in order that the cut will be level when the pony is being ridden. The length of the tail can have an effect on the overall picture and you can only learn this with experience.

Native ponies tails should only be very carefully tidied up by pulling out any straggly hairs. If the end is very long and your breed society does not specifically forbid it, you can shorten the tail a little by using an old clipper blade or a special 'tail knife', taking care that the overall effect is completely natural. Some breed societies – Shetland for example – forbid this, even if the tail is trailing on the ground, so do check before you lop anything off.

If your pony has a really unruly tail, you can help to tame it by bandaging nightly, making sure that the bandage is not too tight. This applies to pulled tails and those which will require plaiting.

CHAPTER SEVEN

Management of the Hunter Pony

CARE AND FEEDING

A working hunter pony should be in show condition, and be fit enough to jump round a course of jumps, then do a ridden and an in-hand show. A show hunter pony will not have to jump but will still have to do a ridden show and probably an in-hand one too. This is, of course, coupled with travel, standing in the lorry at the showground and so on. Some ponies lose condition very quickly while others will do a long day at a show and still look good the next day. It is a question of getting to know your pony and adjusting your management strategy accordingly.

There are many good books available on feeding and nutrition but here are a few general guidelines which may help to set you on the right tracks. Firstly, children's ponies and native ponies should never be kept stabled all the time. The system which has best suited almost all of the ponies which we have ever had is a regime of out in the daytime and in at night, with this possibly reversed in very hot summer weather. The exception to this would be the unfortunate pony who suffers from laminitis; such an animal might be better confined in a stable or even in a small bare paddock for most of the time.

If you have poor grazing or your pony is not carrying enough condition, he should have a good haynet at night in the summer and ad-lib hay available during the winter. Good meadow hay is excellent food for ponies and some do very well on this alone. However, most ponies, in order to perform well and do enough work to attain a suitable level of fitness, need their diet to contain some 'hard' (concentrate) food. This can either be in the form of specially formulated cubes or coarse mix (very useful for inexperienced owners who can just follow the directions on the bag) or a range of 'straights' which you can mix yourself.

The feeding of ponies is very much a skill learnt with experience. Some ponies respond badly to grain feeds such as oats, barley and maize. The reason for this can either be that they are simply receiving too much energy for the job, or that fermentation in the large intestine causes a rise in glucose and other constituents in the blood, which in turn raises the metabolic rate and therefore literally 'heats' up the animal.

There are a number of other foods such as sugar-beet, bran and chaff which can be used to form the basis of a mixed ration.

Show animals need a high percentage of oil in their diet and this can easily be added by feeding half to a full cup of sunflower oil per day. Linseed also has a high oil content, but should be thoroughly boiled before feeding.

Common Feedstuffs

• **Oats** – Oats are actually a very good feed for horses. They are high in fibre and low in energy. (Yes, you did read that correctly!) Oats and other so-called 'heating' feeds only cause problems when they are fed in excess relative to the work being done and by the process of fermentation in the large intestine referred to above. Boiling oats and other grains makes them more digestible and largely counteracts the effects of fermentation. Oats are great for sprinkling on the top of the feed of a fussy eater.

• **Barley** – Barley contains more starch than oats, and this is why boiled barley is a traditional conditioner for poor doers. Barley actually has a higher energy content than oats and has been known to cause various allergic reactions, such as protein rash and leg problems.

• **Sugar-beet** – This is an excellent and very cheap feed for ponies. Being the dried residue left after sugar is extracted from beet, it is sweet and tasty. Since it has to be carefully soaked overnight in plenty of water, it is also useful for dampening the feed. Sugar-beet pulp also has the benefit of being high in fibre. Sugar-beet pulp which has been soaked can ferment in warm weather and attract flies and should therefore be soaked freshly on a daily basis and kept in a shady place.

• **Bran** – Sadly it is not really possible to get good broad bran these days, but nevertheless bran is a useful bulking agent for greedy ponies. Too much bran should not be fed, particularly to young horses, as it prevents the uptake of calcium from other sources. A warm bran mash is very comforting for a tired horse, and a bran mash made with sugar-beet water is good for a sick animal. It can be useful for 'disguising' medicine, and a few oats can be sprinkled on the top to start the pony eating.

• **Chaff** – Chaff is another great feed for greedy ponies. Today you can buy chaff with or without various added ingredients, such as alfalfa, molasses and herbs. Chaff helps to bulk out the feed and slow down eating. You can simply feed chaff with a ready mixed feedstuff and you will usually have a very satisfactory ration.

There are several factors you should consider when planning your feeding:

1 Look at your pony and decide if he is too fat, too thin or just right. Maybe you could weigh him, either on a weighbridge or with a weigh tape, and then calculate exactly how much you need to feed him. His temperament and age should also be taken into consideration. As a rough guide, a 14hh pony, who would measure about 65in./165cm round the girth and weigh around 830lbs/375kg would require about 18lbs/8.5kg of dry matter (not hard food!) per day. If part of this were grass, which is 75% water, obviously the actual bulk of the food would be much more than if the pony was only being fed hay and concentrates which have a much lower water content.

2 Are you feeding him for competition or just for maintenance in the 'off season'? Is he clipped or unclipped? – the clipped pony needs more food just to keep warm and maintain his weight. If he is turned out in a New Zealand rug in the winter, he will still need an increase in food. If you find he is very tired after a competition, you should increase his energy-food intake. If he is too 'hot' in competition, then you should decrease his grain.

3 Does he naturally do well (in which case he is probably a native!) or is he a picky eater or poor doer? Can you give him

something to encourage his appetite (presumably you will have checked that he is not ill and that he does not have worms or tooth problems)? Carrots and apples encourage a poor eater, as does the herb fenugreek.

4 Have you got good grazing – or perhaps even none at all? It is possible to keep ponies on very little grass, but being able to turn them out for most of the day will not only save time, in the amount of mucking out time needed, but will also save money and provide a much more natural diet. If you have a lot of grass in the summer it is possible to cut it, in long lengths, and feed it in a haynet either in the night or at shows, just like you would feed hay. This is a useful way to feed a horse who will not drink at a show, because at least he will get some moisture from the grass. Another useful idea for horses who will not drink or those who get very tired is to soak some sugar-beet in lots of water and then strain off the water for the pony to drink. It will be full of sugar and a bit like a person having a drink of Lucozade!

5 Water is very important. Clean fresh water should be available at all times. Ponies will often not drink if the water is stale or if it has hay in it. If you have a very sensitive pony, it is always better to take water from home to offer to him at a show. Some ponies will not drink 'strange' water and some can even suffer colic from a change in water. Ponies sometimes change coat colour slightly when they change home; this is nothing to worry about and is merely due to the various minerals and so on in the water. (A dramatic change in coat colour would usually signal some serious problem and should be investigated by your vet.)

6 Most ponies can live on good hay alone. Good hay should be greenish brown in colour and smell sweet. There should be no dust or mould in it. Meadow hay (which is made from permanent pasture) is the best for ponies. It should be checked for poisonous plants such as ragwort and buttercups. If one bale has any such plant in it, you can bet that others will and the whole consignment would be better discarded. Ponies will benefit from the mixture of herbs that is in good meadow hay and which is not present in seed hay. Seed hay is made from purposely sown fields. It is of a coarse, sometimes straw-like appearance and is usually higher in protein than meadow hay.

Haylage, which is now widely available, is a good (although

often expensive) alternative forage for ponies with coughing problems. It is made by sealing semi-wilted grass into airtight plastic bags. During storage, the grass ferments slightly. Little ponies love haylage and care must be taken not to let them overeat.

Wetting hay for feeding to ponies who have breathing problems is a controversial subject. It used to be thought that haynets should be immersed in hot water and left there soaking overnight, to counteract the harmful fungal spores which caused the allergy. Nowadays, it is thought that this is not necessary and a five-minute soak in cold water is advised. If you have really good hay, this should be enough, but if you have any doubts, and your pony is a 'serious' cougher, then you would be safest to plump for haylage.

Supplements and herbs

There are many supplements on the market and new ones are appearing all the time. If you feed pony cubes or a coarse mix the feed should contain the proper balance of nutrients and you should not need to feed anything else. Some supplements such as selenium, for example, can be harmful if fed in excess – although if your horse has a deficiency he will need it made up. (If you have any doubts, consult your veterinary surgeon.)

Herbs can be useful and safe supplements for a number of conditions. A few which your working hunter pony might find useful are listed below:

• **Garlic:** Brilliant for ponies with respiratory problems. It can also help towards the prevention of laminitis and skin problems.

• **Stinging nettle:** Good fed internally for skin problems; it can also be used as a final conditioning rinse for improving the coat, mane and tail.

• **Dandelion:** Any pony who has ever had laminitis should have a handful of fresh, or half a handful of dried, dandelion leaves every day.

• **Fenugreek:** The best conditioner and appetiser of all.

• **Kelp:** Rich in minerals, this is a good, safe supplement for ponies who are on poor grazing. It can also help promote hoof growth.

• **Mint:** Useful for the pony who gets nervous in competition. It will help his digestion and guard against 'nervous colic'.

• **Chamomile:** This is suitable for the pony who is nervous or highly strung. It can also be combined with valerian. You can use three chamomile tea bags to make him a pint of tea and pour it over his feed. If you have a nervous rider, he or she should have a big mug of chamomile tea about half an hour before the competition, but do make sure that they also know where the toilet is!

FEET AND SHOES

Everyone has heard the old saying 'No foot – no horse', and it really is true. Your hunter pony, whether he wears shoes or not, needs the services of a good blacksmith. Corrective shoeing can do much to enhance the action of a pony, and good level feet always look better aesthetically.

A good farrier will put on an appropriate weight of shoe for the size of the pony. However, if your pony has a high knee action (and he is not a native breed which allows this) you can have lightweight shoes put on the front to ensure that his shoes

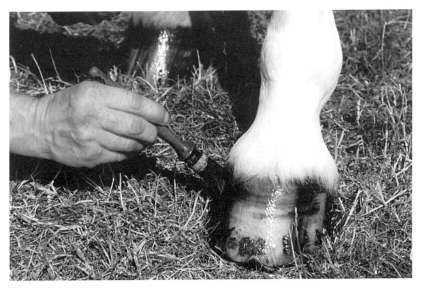

Applying hoof oil enhances the look of a neat, well-shod foot.

75

do not make him lift his knees even higher.

If you have your pony shod too frequently, or if you have a poor farrier or your pony loses shoes often, you will have lots of nail holes in the feet, which do not look tidy. A farriery appointment every five or six weeks should work quite well for most ponies, and this should allow at least some of the nail holes and any small chips or cracks to be removed with the trimming. Do not let your pony's feet get too long, though, as it may cause tripping and stumbling – and does not look smart either.

If you want to use studs, ask your farrier to put stud holes in both sides of the shoe, and make sure that the studs are removed and the holes plugged after use. Do not use studs on hard ground or on the road (unless they are special road studs) because this will jar the pony's joints.

It is perfectly possible to show little ponies unshod. Ponies without shoes are always safer around little children anyway. Nevertheless, the feet should be attended to regularly by the farrier. It will help to keep a pony's feet tidy, if you buy yourself a rasp and at the first sign of a chip or crack, you just file it off, as you might do for your own nails. You should not, however, attempt to do any more than this.

Bad feet should be coated regularly with a proprietary product to improve hoof growth. Supplements containing biotin are also thought to help. A young pony should have a proper amount of calcium in his diet. Normally a pony out at grass gets enough calcium (needed for proper skeletal development) from the grazing, but if a pony is on restricted grazing or receiving a diet which includes a high proportion of concentrates, you may need a supplement. A calcium supplement is especially important for ponies who have had or have laminitis.

When your farrier visits, you can ask him to trim the chest-nuts, if they are protruding. The chestnut is formed from dead cells, like the hoof. However, it is better not to try and trim them yourself as you need a very sharp knife and you would not want to slip and cut the pony's leg.

WORMING AND TEETH

You need to keep any show animal in the very best of condition so attention should be paid to worming. If you are able to move your ponies around and graze them alternately with other animals such as sheep or cattle, then worming can be done twice a year. If, as most people, you only have a set area of grazing, then worming will need to be done more often – six weeks being the recommended interval. If you have just one small paddock, then droppings should be picked up regularly.

Teeth can be checked by the vet, when the annual vaccinations are done, but if there are any signs of tooth problems then attention should be sought as soon as possible. Tooth problems manifest in dropping food; in bit problems; in holding the head to one side; in loss of condition; and in various other more subtle ways. Wolf teeth sometimes grow in front of the premolars. If these interfere with the bit or if they are loose and cause the pony problems, they should be removed. Although there is no scientific evidence that the removal of wolf teeth causes miracles to occur, it is true that in many ponies a significant effect is noted.

VACCINATIONS

Vaccinations for flu and tetanus (especially tetanus) are sensible and are also essential for entry to some shows. They should be done at a time when the pony is having his annual rest. They can cause a reaction in some sensitive animals, and for this reason you should obey the guidelines issued by your vet as to how long the pony should rest after vaccination. You will need to obtain a certificate and to keep it in a safe place. The recommended intervals between vaccinations change as more is known about the effects, so you should check with your vet as to current thinking.

MEASUREMENT

All ponies shown under British Show Pony Society rules and at the finals of National Pony Society competitions require a height certificate. It is also a useful document to have when you sell a pony, as the height is clearly stated. Measurement is done under the Joint Measurement Scheme (see address list), by specially appointed veterinary surgeons and at an appointed place. You will have to book an appointment and then take your pony to the measuring pad. He should not be wearing shoes. There are two types of certificate, annual and life, and the Joint Measurement Scheme rules will explain which you need.

STABLING AND STABLE MANAGEMENT

The first thing that you have to consider with a hunter pony is whether or not you want to produce him yourself. There are plenty of professional yards up and down the country who will do all the work for you, so that you just have to arrive at the show with your immaculate child and plonk him or her on board. Personally I feel that this is missing out on the fun. After all, anyone can do it, if they have enough money – but to bring on and look after your ponies yourself and then have success is much more rewarding. So the rest of this section is for those of you who want to 'do it yourselves'.

If you do not have stables and paddocks attached to your house, you will have to put your pony in a livery yard, but you can still do most of the work yourself, especially if you have a DIY livery arrangement – which means in effect that you just rent the field and stable. If you have your own facilities, then this is the very best system, although of course you will be tied down somewhat. We arrange for our ponies to go to a livery yard when we go on holiday. This means that we can go away without wondering if they are all right being looked after by friends or relatives, because we know they will be getting professional care; and it also means that they have a change of scene, which is good for anyone. If you can arrange a holiday and take your ponies with you, this may also work.

You cannot really show any horse or pony without at least having access to a stable. If you have an early class and white socks then you will really need to do things the day before and preserve the results of your efforts!

Whether you use straw for bedding or shavings, paper or hemp is often a matter of availability. Ponies who cough on straw should always be bedded on shavings, paper or hemp. Shavings can sometimes be difficult to dispose of – for some reason gardeners do not seem to like them. Paper blows about in the yard. Hemp is easy to manage but more expensive. You just have to experiment and see what suits you best, but always

A shiny coat and a good covering of flesh indicate the good condition of this pony.

ensure that the bed is deep enough to guard against injury. Capped hocks will not enhance your chances in the ring.

The door of a show animal's stable is important. If the door is too high your pony is in danger of developing a muscle underneath the neck from continually stretching to see over the top. For the same reason, the haynet should not be hung too high. If the pony is small and there is a danger of him catching his leg in a net, then it is better to feed the hay on the floor.

It goes without saying that everything in your stable and field should be safe. This includes fencing, gates and water troughs. There are ponies who will injure themselves given even the smallest sharp protrusion, so regular checking of your pony's environment and equipment is vital. If you have a lovely pony and he gets a noticeable scar – or, worse still, permanently lames himself – because you did not check everything properly, you will never forgive yourself. It is all too easy to glance at your fences and assume that just because they are still standing they must be OK. You should go round regularly and actually test the rails and the posts, and nail up anything which is beginning to come loose, thus saving yourself future problems. Whilst on this subject, barbed wire is not a suitable fencing for horses. The best cheap or temporary solution is electric fencing, but do ensure that you set it up safely, according to the manufacturer's directions.

If you have a pony whose temperament is better suited to plenty of time outdoors, you will probably need to think about providing a field shelter, so that by use of this and rugging him up well, he can spend most of the daylight hours outside, even in the winter. Ponies who might need this treatment would include those with stable vices and those who are a fizzy ride if kept stabled too long.

Any doubts about your pony's legs can be overcome by turning him out in exercise boots, but these should be securely taped on, otherwise you will spend hours searching for them when he loses them somewhere in the long grass.

If you have to leave a headcollar on your pony, because he is sometimes difficult to catch, you should be careful to ensure that it fits properly and will not rub. There are various quick-release headcollars on the market which will break if the pony gets caught up in anything, or if you are worried, you can replace one of the metal rings in your headcollar with a loop of twine, which will of course break much more easily than your pony's neck, if he gets caught on the fencing.

Crib-biters and windsuckers should be given plenty of variety in their lives and anything which they may be able to grab should be removed or coated in a proprietary deterrent. A collar can be used, but care should be taken not to damage the mane. The new 'Miracle Collars', if correctly fitted, seem to be pretty effective against both vices.

Weavers should have proper weaving bars fitted to their stable door, and they should be out in the paddock as much as possible. A pony who weaves can damage his joints through the constant movement.

RUGS AND RUGGING UP

Sadly, some poor ponies never actually feel the sun on their backs at all – it is not an uncommon sight to see show ponies sweltering in their rugs, whilst tied to a lorry at a show, in the middle of summer. This cannot improve their temperament.

When trying to decide whether or not your pony needs a rug, there is one very good rule-of-thumb which may help you: if you need a coat on, then so will your pony; if you need a thick sweater and a coat, then he will need an under-rug and a top rug; and if you need a waterproof coat... – you get the picture? This general guide does not allow for the very thin-skinned pony who may need an extra rug; nor does it take account of very hot weather, when it is crime to rug up any pony, day or night. A bit of dust in his coat will soon wash out. Even grey ponies need a bit of freedom!

Stable rugs should be well fitting, otherwise they will leave rub marks on the pony's coat – like the bald shoulder patches which are so often seen at the British Show Pony Society Winter Championships. A cotton summer sheet can be used next to the skin, so that this can be changed when it has absorbed grease and dirt. This will therefore save you having to wash thicker rugs too often.

The clipped pony needs to be well rugged up, to avoid loss of condition. If he has a full clip, he may also need a hood on colder nights. He should be exercised with a woollen quarter sheet to cover his loins. New Zealand rugs can rub a clipped pony's legs where the leg straps make contact. If this is the case, put Vaseline or a similar greasy substance on the inside of the straps when putting the rug on. You really do need to have two New Zealand rugs if you are using them every day. It is very difficult to put on a wet, muddy New Zealand and it will also be very uncomfortable and heavy for the pony.

Hoods are very useful, both for clipped ponies (as mentioned) and for keeping a pony clean for a show. They come in several types and styles. Possibly the most useful is made of stretchy material and is opened by a zip along the underside of the neck. Hoods usually fasten to the rug to stop them slipping. You can also get quilted hoods, which will help to keep the coat growth rate down in cold weather – this is something you may want to do, for example, if your pony has qualified for one of the winter shows or the British Show Pony Society Winter Championships.

They can make a pony very hot if the weather is not cold enough to warrant them and should therefore be checked when in use. Waterproof hoods that attach to New Zealand rugs are a boon for those of us who own grey or other light-coloured ponies with a penchant for rolling. They save much cleaning up work. However, they can rub the mane and if this is the case, you can use a tighter fitting stretchy hood underneath. You can also put some conditioner on the mane every day, so that the hood tends to slide over the hair. The only problem with this is that when you need to plait, it does take some washing out. If you have a native pony, however, this will help to make his mane easier to handle.

Some people bandage their ponies' legs in the winter to keep them warm and deter the coat growth. It must be pretty awful standing around all day with your legs bandaged, to say nothing of being downright dangerous in the field. If you are worried about your pony having hairy legs you can apply a thin coating of gel down the legs after bathing to smooth down the hair; alternatively, you can clip early and hope that not too much grows.

A final word on management

To keep your pony sweet, do not make the mistake of showing him every single week. It must be so boring for ponies who get this kind of treatment. There are many other events and competitions that a pony can do, to say nothing of hunting in the winter and Pony Club in the summer – so there can be no excuse for not giving your pony lots of variety. Some ponies shown from professional yards do tend to get 'overshown', but if you show your pony from home you will probably be constrained by other factors and not be tempted to do this anyway.

CHAPTER EIGHT

Tack and Clothing

BRIDLES

Most classes will allow any bit and bridle. However, there are some items which are just not used in these classes. These include gags of any kind; nosebands with strange rubber contraptions hanging from them; and hackamore (bitless) bridles. A pony with a double bridle, wrapped round with a flash noseband and secured with a tight standing martingale, will not get many points for manners, but in an open class, a pony going sweetly in a double bridle looks very nice. Snaffles are usually the rule in a novice class, and a running martingale should not be penalised, although it must always be used with rein stops correctly fitted.

The bridle should be the right weight for the size of pony, and generally it should appear workmanlike rather than thin and showy. Everything should fit well, and be the correct size for the pony. All the buckles on the bridle should fasten on the middle holes or thereabouts. Long flapping straps look awful, even if they are in the keepers. The fit of a bridle can do much to enhance the appearance of the head.

All the pieces of the bridle should match in colour of leather and in weight – that is, in the width and thickness of the leather. It does look better if all your buckles are the same, although a slight variation in buckle shape does not usually show. Buckles should be stainless steel; brass buckles do not look right in any showing class.

Bits should fit and be of stainless steel. A child who needs a pelham bit can have split reins if he or she cannot manage two reins. Split reins consist of a rein which goes to the top ring of the bit and a shorter piece of rein (or a long cheekpiece) which is buckled to the bottom ring of the bit at the billet end, the end that would have buckled to the headpiece being slid over the main rein and then buckled onto holes which are punched in that rein at the appropriate place (which is usually around 6-8in./15-20cm) from the bit. A slight adjustment can then be made to the action of the bottom 'rein' if necessary. Any good saddler should be able to make these for you – they look much smarter than pelham roundings. Any bit with a curb chain or leather curb should have a lip strap properly fitted.

Browbands should be plain – never velvet-covered or brassed, although a leather plaited or stitched insert would be acceptable.

Split reins are much neater than pelham roundings.

A well-fitted double bridle.

Nosebands should be plain leather and if you need the action of a drop noseband, then use a flash, which looks much smarter. The fit of a noseband can greatly change the appearance of a head. If your pony has a very plain head, a Grakle can sometimes be worn to good effect. If he has a long face, a wide, flat noseband will have the effect of cutting the head in half and thus making it look better. In fact, a wide, flat, plain noseband does wonders for almost any head.

A drop noseband fitted somewhere around the nostrils will make any head look long and plain.

If you use a flash noseband with the top part in the usual place for a normal cavesson (i.e. just below the bottom of the cheek bones) then the bottom part will usually be in the right place. This should be adjusted so that the pony cannot open his mouth, but can still breathe.

Reins should be leather, although a dark-coloured rubber lining is useful in wet weather. Plaited or laced leather reins look good and provide a degree of grip. Small children's reins should not be so long that the rider can catch his or her foot – or, worse still, the pony's foot – in them.

Rein stops for running martingales should be leather or dark rubber – NOT pink! This also applies to the rubber on a running martingale.

SADDLES

Firstly it should be said that breastplates, overgirths, cruppers and other saddle-holding devices are not correct for the show ring. The only exception might be a crupper on a very round Shetland competing in mountain and moorland classes. You will just have to get a saddle that fits! If you do have a problem with the saddle slipping forward, a useful option is to have point straps fitted. These are actually girth straps which run from the points of the tree down to the girth. They hold the front of the saddle firmly behind the (fat) wither and shoulders, and on some ponies can actually make the shoulder look better.

If money is no object, you can buy a made-to-measure working hunter pony saddle. This is straight cut, like a show saddle, but has full-length knee rolls (and occasionally small thigh rolls as well). It should have a good deep seat and either a straight or cut-back pommel. The cantle should be high enough for jumping but not too high. The colour should be dark, and ideally it should match the bridle. Often there are no keepers for the excess stirrup leather on working hunter saddles, but this is easily solved by lying the excess leather straight down with the stirrup. Suede saddles are sometimes seen but do look best on show ponies and hacks. Suede knee patches are acceptable.

If you cannot run to a tailor-made working hunter saddle, you can compromise with a show saddle, which will be harder to sit on for the jumping phase, but still the next best choice.

The last choice of all would be a general-purpose saddle, because the knee rolls usually come too far forward and hide the

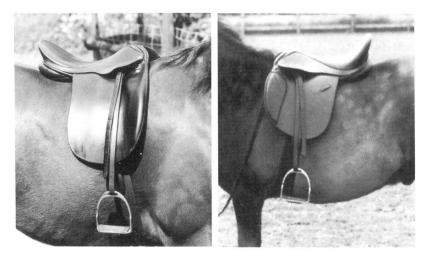

LEFT: A good saddle, with a cut-back head and straight panel.
RIGHT: This saddle is too forward cut and therefore hides the pony's shoulder.

pony's shoulder to some degree. Dressage saddles do some-times fit the larger ponies, but the flap often seems to be too long and does not look right at all.

Whatever saddle you have, it should fit the pony. If you have any doubts about your ability to fit a saddle correctly, ask a qualified saddler to do this for you. A badly fitting saddle may pinch the back and cause jumping problems. The saddle should also fit the rider. With working hunter saddles having smaller knee rolls than general-purpose saddles, you sometimes find that the child's leg comes off the front of the saddle, which looks untidy. If this is the case, the saddle is too small for the rider's length of leg and it will probably be too small in the seat as well. If the rider is not comfortable and balanced in the right part of the saddle, he cannot possibly be expected to ride to the best of his ability.

Girths should be brown, black or white depending on the colour of the pony. If you are using a cotton girth it should obvi-ously be clean (launder it in the washing machine tied inside and old pillowcase). Another alternative is a leather girth, but this must be well cared for to keep it soft and supple and to avoid girth galls. If you need a numnah, then it should be sheep-skin (or imitation sheepskin); it should not extend noticeably beyond the saddle. Like the girth, it should be brown, black or white, depending on the colour of the pony. Never ever use a protruding saddle cloth with the pony's name embroidered on it, or anything else which shows beyond the saddle.

Stirrups should be of stainless steel; safety stirrups are perfectly acceptable for smaller children. Treads should be black or white to match other items. Leathers should be proportionate to the size of the saddle and the rider and neither too wide nor too narrow. Great lengths of unused leather should either be cut off or the leathers changed for shorter ones. A saddler can eas-ily shorten stirrups from the buckle end, which also means that you will have new stitching for a while – which is always safer.

BOOTS

Some rules now allow protective boots to be worn in the jump-ing phase of the class. If you have checked this and they are allowed, then your boots should tone with the pony's colour (e.g. black boots for a dark pony, or white ones for a grey or one with white socks). They should be of the Woof-type of schooling boot, which cover the cannon bone area and wrap round, securing with velcro straps. Such things as fetlock boots, bandages of any kind and over-reach boots are not allowed. If taping boots in place, use matching tape and wind it round neatly.

GENERAL RULES FOR TACK

Tack should always be well fitting and beautifully clean. It must be leather – the new synthetic tack is not permissible. The overall effect should be smart and workmanlike. It should all look as if it belongs to that pony. Nothing should be coloured, including reins, numnahs and so on. Everything should be checked regularly for safety. It is worth considering having two lots of tack, if finances permit – one for best and one for everyday use. Your show tack can then be kept clean and will last much longer. Also, if your child tends to throw his everyday bridle on the stable floor etc., then at least it will not be your show one that suffers. However, if you ride at home, say, in a snaffle and keep your best double bridle for showing, then do ride your poor pony in it a couple of times before a show, so that he remembers how it feels.

TACK CLEANING

Whilst the general methods of tack cleaning do apply to your show tack, there are some tips which may help you. It is all too easy to think that it is enough to clean your tack once or more at every show, but this really will not suffice. To prove this, take it all apart every so often and give it a really thorough clean and you will notice the difference.

To clean leather tack, dismantle every part and wash with warm water and a sponge. For really dirty leather, use a soft nail brush and scrub gently. Dry each item immediately with an old towel and then apply a coating of neatsfoot oil or other similar tack oil. When this has soaked in, polish everything up with saddle soap using as little water as possible. Then reassemble.

The bit should be washed well in plain warm water and scrubbed if necessary with a brush. Some people like to use metal polish on bits, but since this must leave an unpleasant taste in your pony's mouth, its use cannot be recommended. If you have really bad marks or stains, try using a kitchen scourer.

Rubber reins and martingale stops can have a little bit a glycerine rubbed into them to preserve them. The reins should then be rubbed with a dry cloth to ensure that they do not slip through the rider's hands when they are next used.

Saddles should be stripped occasionally and thoroughly cleaned and oiled, making sure that you get the oil right up under the flaps and into all the little cracks and crevices. After saddle soaping everything, the top should be well rubbed with a dry cloth to remove any excess soap and/or oil which would be certain to transfer itself to the rider's jodhpurs. At this time check all the stitching right up under the flaps and the general 'roadworthiness' of the saddle. Look at the stuffing and see if it has gone flat or is lumpy in places. If you are in any doubt, get your saddler to check it for you.

Stirrup leathers can be treated in the same way, and this is a good opportunity to check the stitching. Stirrups can be cleaned either by washing, as for bits, or by buffing up with a little metal polish, if you really want to.

Leather girths should be oiled very regularly, and folded leather girths should have a cloth soaked in oil kept in the centre. Sweat is very acidic and should always be washed off any leather tack as soon as possible.

BITS AND BITTING

No book can possibly tell you which bit to use for your pony. If you are unsure you will really need to consult an expert. However, there are some basic points to consider. Always start ponies off in a snaffle bit. For young children and/or ponies a cheek snaffle helps with steering and also lies quietly in the mouth without rubbing or pulling through. If you need a stronger action but want to stay with a snaffle, then a French link (sometimes called double-jointed) bit will add action on the tongue. There is a type of double-jointed snaffle called a Dr Bristol, which has a central plate, set at an angle. This has a much more severe action.

Pelham and other curb bits come in many shapes and sizes and with mouthpieces in metal, vulcanite, rubber and the new synthetic materials. A bit which sometimes works well for a

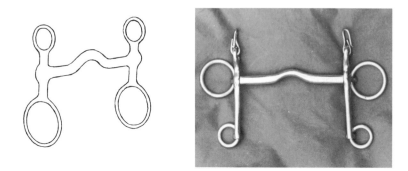

strong, small pony is the globe cheek pelham, which is a curb bit, but with only one rein. A straight or ported mouthpiece is usual with cheeks which consist of a small ring at the top for the cheekpieces and a larger ring at the bottom for the reins. The curb action of this bit can be mitigated by use of a leather curb.

A double bridle always looks good on older ponies (never use a double on a young pony before he is going well in a snaffle) and with older children, if the ponies go well in it. One possible compromise if your pony cannot take a double bridle is the Rugby pelham (sometimes called a showing bit). This has only one mouthpiece, either jointed or straight, and cheeks rather like those of a pelham, but the top bit ring is attached to the mouthpiece in such a way that when the bit is in the mouth it does look like a double bridle.

RIDER'S CLOTHING

All working hunter riders wear tweed, except in evening performances of championships, when they may be asked to wear navy or black. Show hunter pony riders wear tweed, but black or navy at major shows. Tweed jackets can be of a blue, green or brown mixture, the colour chosen to go well with the pony. Generally, grey ponies look well with a blue tweed jacket, for example.

Nearly all rules call for a British Standards skull cap or other BSI-approved hat. Please check the rule book for the exact requirements. The skull cap should be covered by a plain velvet cover in a dark colour which tones with the jacket, usually black or navy.

A shirt with a proper collar, in a tone which matches the jacket, should be worn, together with a plain or discreetly patterned (small spots, for example) matching tie. It is possible to buy some very nice shirts, together with a matching tie and sometimes a hair band too. This kind of ensemble does help the overall effect of smartness.

Jodhpurs or breeches should be fawn or beige. If jodhpurs are worn they should be held down with the special clips which are available at tack shops and shows.

The rider's boots should be leather and either brown or black, depending on the colour scheme chosen. Generally, short boots are worn in working hunter classes and for small children in show hunter classes, but older children and adults riding native ponies can wear long boots. At the present time, none of the rules permit the wearing of spurs in any class.

Buttonholes are not usually worn and the badge of the society under whose rules you are competing is sufficient decoration for the lapel. Wedding-style flowers look really silly!

Gloves should match your boots and can be leather or one of the new synthetics. They should be plain, not white string or brightly coloured pimple-palmed etc. You can either carry a cane or a whip or no stick at all. Some rules stipulate a maximum length of stick. If you qualify for one of the championship finals you will need a proper hunting whip. Although this could be used in an ordinary class, in practice you hardly ever see them.

A smart line-up of show hunter ponies.

When warming up for your class beware of riding your pony in spurs, draw reins or the like. Some rules do not allow the pony to be ridden on the showground in anything other than the tack which is allowed in the class.

All your showing clothes should be washed or dry cleaned as appropriate and well pressed. Leather gloves can be cleaned with saddle soap or glove wash, and cotton gloves should be washed in lukewarm water. Boots should be cleaned and polished, and for added shine can be glossed up with one of the new proprietary wipes or liquids which add a long-lasting lustre.

Children can wear chaps over their jodhpurs until just before they go into the class, to keep them clean – chaps also provide a layer for warmth in cold weather. Spare jodhpurs are always useful with small children, as are spare gloves for anyone riding in bad weather.

Two very important factors about clothing which sometimes get overlooked, especially with children, are that everything should (a) fit the rider, and (b) be comfortable to ride in. For example, if a jacket restricts arm movement, a rider might not be able to adopt the correct position for jumping and so could hamper the pony. Anything which is too tight or which rubs or pinches is bound to be a distraction. Always try out new clothes at home before they are worn in the ring.

Children's, or rather girls', hair is a tricky subject. Long permed hair, garnished with a big bunch of ribbons, is for show pony classes only. Short hair, unless it is very short, should be held in a hair net of a colour which matches the hair. Longer hair can be plaited and folded up into a hair scrunch, bun net or other 'hair restraining' device. Little girls still look very sweet with two plaits adorned by matching ribbons. The overall desired effect is one of being neat and tidy. Earrings and other jewellery are downright dangerous around horses. Make-up should only worn by older girls and adults.

In leading rein classes the handler should be smartly and suitably dressed. Women should wear a jacket and skirt or culottes. Shoes should be flat and comfortable to run in. Hats should be of the plain felt variety – not flowery wedding confections. Everything should match and tone in with the rider's attire. Men should wear a dark suit. A shirt and/or tie which matches that worn by the rider, looks very smart.

CHAPTER NINE

Show Day

PAPERWORK

Some shows have entries which close long before the day of the show (although some do have entries on the day) and you will need to check this well in advance. In the early part of the year, *Horse and Hound* publishes a comprehensive list of shows. Keep a note of the shows that you want to enter and the closing dates for entries, and make sure that you send for the schedule in good time. Smaller shows will accept entries on the day, but at county level it will be a complete waste of time trying to enter even one day after the closing date.

If you are waiting for passes and/or tickets to arrive in the post, do not leave it until less than a week before the show to advise the organiser that they have not arrived. If there has been an administrative error at the show office, or your tickets have been lost in the post, they will need time to post another set.

When entering a show, fill in the forms correctly and remember to enclose your cheque. Many shows will not accept half-filled-out entry forms and, even if they return your entry for amendment, you may well then miss the closing date.

Never try to enter a class for which you are not eligible – this is cheating!

If you are showing under British Show Pony Society rules, you will have had your pony officially measured, joined the Society and registered the pony. For National Pony Society qualifying classes, the rider and owner of the pony must be members and the pony must have a competition record card. Other societies have different criteria and it is no good looking at these things the day before the show or, worse, on the day of the show itself.

Keep a file for taking to shows, and the day before you set off, put everything which applies to that particular show inside it. This means height and vaccination certificates, if they are needed; your number and passes, if they are issued before the show; and your copy of the schedule. A little time spent on these administrative preparations will always be well spent. At every show there is at least one person who does not have the right papers and has therefore had a wasted journey.

If you have a computer you can devise a simple programme to help you with your entries. You could use a file for each pony and enter his details, including registration numbers, dates for vaccinations, worming and so on, then just call up his file whilst doing your entries and all the details are to hand.

This is perhaps a good point to mention that all ponies should be properly insured against third-party risks. If, say, a rider falls off in a class and the pony gets loose on the showground, it could result in a claim for many thousands of pounds. Membership of some organisations, such as the Pony Club and the British Horse Society, automatically includes third-party cover, but you should check this before you go to any show.

WHAT TO TAKE

Preparation is the key to a happy day at a show – whether you are successful or not! If you have a lorry, then many items can be stored there and just checked the day before the show. It really pays to have a 'show' grooming box which is left ready from one show to the next. Things to remember to pack fall into several categories and suggested lists for each are given below.

PROVISIONS

- **Haynet** (and spare hay on long days).

- **Water bucket** and sufficient **water** for the pony to drink and for washing etc. Some showgrounds do not have water available.

- **Feed** and **feeding bucket** or manger.

- **Provisions for people.** There is not always a catering van and even if there is, you may prefer to take your own food and drink.

TACK AND RUGS

- **Saddle and bridle** and other bits/bridles if different ones are used in different classes. **Spare clean girth**.

- **Martingale** (if used).

- **Boots** – include some spare travelling boots or bandages in case the first set gets wet (in long grass or from 'natural causes'!).

- **Waterproof sheet** (and hood) for wet weather

- **Quarter sheet** in cold weather.

- **Sweat sheet** or cooler.

- **Spare rugs**/sheets and hood. Those large plastic storage boxes that are available in DIY stores can be very useful if you have to remove your things from the vehicle after each show, and for storing spare rugs.

GROOMING KIT

- **Brushes** (including clean body brush and separate brush for white socks if you use chalk).

- **Cloths** (including a sponge or flannel which can be used wet for removing marks).

- **Plaiting kit** and scissors; **hair gel** or other smoothing agent; **spare needles** (so that two people can plait at once if time is short).

- **Quarter markers**, water brush and hairspray (if you use it).

- **Comb.**

- **Tack-cleaning kit** and sponges.

- **Baby oil** and **hoof oil. Fly spray** (if it happens to be that kind of weather).

- **Washing bucket**, plus **soap** or shampoo and some old **towels.**

- **Chalk** (if you need it).

- **Coat conditioning spray.**

- **Ringside kit** in a small tray or bucket. This should include a minimum of a clean cloth and brush and a comb. You will soon learn which items your pony regularly needs.

CLOTHING

- **Jacket, shirt and tie, jodhpurs, boots.**

- **Gloves,** and a spare pair for wet weather.

- **Hat** and hat cover.

- **Hairbrush,** hair accessories and mirror.

- **Jodhpur clips.**

- **Spare jodhpurs**, in case the rider falls off.

- **Chaps** (invaluable for keeping small children warm and comfortable – and they are very nice for older people too!).

- **Waterproof coat.**

- **Shoe-cleaning kit.**

- **Tie pin.**

- **Clothes brush.**

- **Small sewing kit.**

However, these are only suggestions and you will have favourite items and other important things to add to the list. If you are the sort of person who always forgets something, make a master checklist and tick off each item or chore on it.

Other Essential Equipment

- All of the necessary **paperwork,** including the numbers if they have been sent to you beforehand; any passes which you might need to gain admission and vaccination certificates if they are required. Make sure everything is to hand so that you don't hold up the queue going into the showground if documents are being inspected there.

- **First aid kits.** One for humans and one for equines. The human one should include wound dressings and antiseptic wipes; pain relief tablets and any prescription drugs which anyone might need. Insect repellent and sting relief cream are also useful in the summer. Add your favourite items to these and check the contents regularly. The horse's first aid should include human antiseptic wipes, which are perfectly safe for horses; wound powder (black for dark coloured horses and white for light coloured ones); bandages, including the invaluable Vetwrap; something like leg ice or Animalintex dressing for sprains and strains and any items which your pony might regularly need.

- A **mobile phone** is very useful for conveying the good news home – and, of course, don't forget the camera for those all-important pictures.

- If you are travelling to a showground that you do not know, be sure to take a good **map.** Sometimes traffic restrictions mean that you have to leave a showground by a different exit and you may well need to consult the map to get back to your route.

TRAVELLING

Whether travelling with a trailer or in a lorry, you must ensure that everything is safe and in good running order. A mechanical breakdown whilst transporting horses is a major problem. There are several roadside rescue organisations which you can join who specialise in horse transport, but there really is no substitute for proper, regular maintenance.

Towing a trailer is a skill which should be practised, with the trailer empty. Both trailers and lorries should never be driven too fast or too roughly. Imagine travelling for an hour or two being thrown about in the back of a lorry and arriving at a strange place, feeling thoroughly seasick and then being expected to perform at your very best. This is what some drivers expect their ponies to do!

Start your journey in plenty of time to allow for the unforseen, such as punctures and traffic problems. And always check that you have sufficient fuel before you set out.

The pony should wear either bandages or boots, a tail bandage and rugs appropriate to the weather. There have been some horrific accidents involving horses travelling without adequate leg protection. In these days when velcro-fastened boots take only a few seconds to put on, there can be no excuse.

The pony's tail can be protected with either a tail bandage or one of the special tail guards which are now on the market. If you have a plaited tail, you will have to use a guard and put it on and take it off carefully.

If it is very hot, a cotton sheet will help your pony to stay clean.

Once on board the trailer or lorry, he should be tied to a piece of string, attached to a tie ring. Leather headcollars are better than nylon ones for travelling, because they break more easily in the event of an accident. Never, ever tie a pony directly to a tie ring by his rope – if you have an accident or if he has a panic, he could easily break his neck. If your pony is a really bad traveller, you should consider using knee boots and a poll guard to protect him. If you have a native pony and are afraid of spoiling his feather by bandaging, you will have to decide whether to risk travelling him unbandaged. Do not try to use loose boots – these are more dangerous than nothing at all.

There should be adequate ventilation in the trailer or lorry. If you arrive at the show with your pony sweated up, you may have difficulty removing the marks and getting the pony dry before the class.

Whether or not you use straw or other bedding on the floor of your lorry or trailer is a matter of personal preference. My ponies have travelled very well on rubber granalistic flooring, without any bedding at all. If you do use straw or shavings, it must be sufficiently deep not to slide around under the ponies' feet, and you should take a strong plastic sack and a pair of rubber gloves for mucking out. Most shows do not allow mucking out onto the showground, and it is polite to clear away any droppings etc. from around the horsebox anyway.

Whether or not you give your pony hay on a journey is dependent on several factors. If he is a bad traveller and going on a long journey, then a haynet may help to settle him. For short journeys, when you are expecting to be competing within, say, the next couple of hours, it is better to withhold the haynet until after the competition. No pony jumps well on a full tummy and if he is a greedy little native, then he will be sure to eat everything which is given to him!

As with the general rules for feeding, he should not have any hard food or a long drink of water for at least an hour before competing (or travelling). A small drink to refresh him when you arrive at the showground is fine.

ON ARRIVAL AT THE SHOW

When you arrive, you should collect your numbers, if they have not been sent in the post before the show, and find out where your ring is. You should also check how far into the schedule the classes have progressed. Armed with this information you should be able to judge approximately how much time you have before your class, to get ready. How long you need is really a matter both of personal preference and of the amount of working in and settling your pony requires. This is something you just have to learn by experience. When you read the schedule never make the mistake of allowing too much time for the classes before you. They are sure to be the classes with only one or two entries, which are over in a matter of minutes. If in doubt it is better to be early!

For working hunter pony classes you will need to watch out for the class before to finish so that you can walk the course at the appropriate time.

If your pony has collected any dirty marks when travelling, or overnight and it was too dark to see when you set off, you can now rectify the matter. Stains can be washed off with a tiny drop of shampoo. If you get lots of soap everywhere, you may have difficulty getting rid of it. An old face flannel makes a very good cloth for rubbing stains away. The pony can then be rubbed with a dry towel, and hopefully any wet areas will begin to dry off whilst you are riding in.

Your pony can be ridden-in wearing his bandages, especially if he has white socks. As stated, he should not wear any tack which is not permitted in the ring, if you are competing under official rules.

When he has worked sufficiently on the flat, and he is competing in a worker or style and performance class, find the practice fence and take him over it two or three times. Do not jump it again and again. This will only tire him and this is NOT the time for schooling. There are people who drape their coat or a rug over the jump. I have never, ever seen a jump in a competition with a coat on it – so what is the point of practising this?

If you intend to plait your pony at the show, do allow more time than you would need at home. The pony may well be more fidgety and there will usually be people coming by for a chat and so on.

About twenty minutes before your class, you can start your final preparations. A good body brushing should be followed by a polish with a clean cloth. This is the time to apply coat conditioner, if you use it. Any loose hairs sticking up from plaits can be stuck down again with gel, and a native mane can be combed out and subdued with gel or hair dressing if necessary. There are numerous products on the market for taming human hair and I recommend that you keep trying them until you find one which suits your pony! The tail bandage can be left on until the collecting ring, but the ends should be uncovered and combed out. Bushy native tails can be tamed as for the mane. Bandages should be removed and white socks re-chalked if necessary. Excess chalk can be brushed out, because if you don't do it, when the pony starts to trot it will sprinkle itself all over the newly oiled hooves.

Quarter markers should be applied to British Show Pony Society ponies, unless they have their winter coat or they are light grey (in which case it is not worth bothering). There are lots of patterns which can be used, and you can buy special marker templates. Experience will teach you what pattern suits your pony. If you use a template, you should hold it securely to the coat, which has been slightly dampened first, and then brush the hairs firmly in the other direction. You can then spray it with hairspray (whilst the template is still in place) so that it will hold when dry.

Alternatively you can do your own. The best tool I have ever used is a piece of plastic comb, cut off to the required length. The coat is then brushed down with a damp water brush and then squares are made by scraping the coat the wrong way with the comb.

The second thigh can be brushed with diamonds by using the water brush first one way and then the other. If your pony has a weak bottom, you can brush the hairs either side of the tail out vertically and then do a large rounded sweep each side to make things look rounder.

Hoof oil can be applied either now or in the collecting ring. In long, wet grass, you are better to leave it as late as possible. Baby oil should be rubbed into the face and muzzle. This has the effect of fining down the face and making the eyes look larger. Never be tempted to use shoe polish or similar things to enlarge the eyes. If the pony gets such a preparation in his eye he could be permanently blinded.

If you have two people – usually in my experience mother and rider – the rider can be getting into his riding clothes whilst the mother/groom gets the pony ready. Check that small children have the right paperwork in their pocket, such as qualification cards and competition cards.

In very wet weather, you should try to keep the pony under cover as much as possible and then ride him to the ring with a

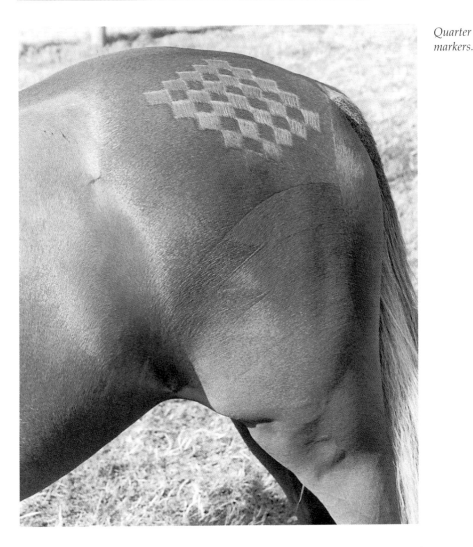

waterproof quarter sheet on. The rider can wear a waterproof coat over his jacket and take it off just as he goes into the ring.

Once the rider is on board, the groom should gather up the groom's kit – and away you go!

After the class, you should immediately untack your pony and put on his sheet. If he has another class to do and has white legs, you will need to refit his leg bandages; you will also need to reapply his tail bandage.

At a show the usual rules about feeding and watering apply; that is to say he should not be fed or watered whilst he is hot. In very hot weather you will have to either tie him up on the shady side of the box or put him back inside the lorry/trailer with the ramp open – if he will stand happily like that. With experience

101

you will know whether your pony needs hard food at a show or not. Some droop badly without enough food, whilst others are better without any.

No matter how tired you are, wrap him up properly to travel home – you may live to regret it if you don't. A very useful pick-me-up for tired ponies is to put the water that sugar-beet has been soaked in into his drinking water. It is full of sugar and will give him some energy. Beware of the pony who will not drink at shows. He may well need to be given electrolytes to help him through the day. Electrolytes also encourage a horse to drink. If you have a pony who is fussy about drinking away from home, take a container of your 'home' water and make sure it is filled freshly each time. Sometimes taking his usual water bucket from home helps. Do not, however, give any pony a long drink just before travelling.

We always give our ponies a couple of days off after shows, to give them a chance to relax. If your pony has been really stressed at a show, he will benefit from a bran mash on arrival home, possibly made up with chamomile tea. It is part of having horses that you always see to them first when you get home – besides which if you sit down with a cup of tea after a long day at a show, you will never get up again!

CHAPTER TEN

Judges, Judging and Marking

To BE a judge is to hold a position of great power. After all, judges can make your day – or completely ruin it – so what can we as competitors expect from them?

Firstly, if you are showing under the rules of one of the main societies, you can expect the judge to be on the society's panel of approved judges. (Incidentally, the coursebuilder will be someone from their approved panel too, under British Show Pony Society rules.) Judges are accepted onto these panels in a variety of ways. They may judge a particular breed and have been through one of the breed societies' training and assessment days. They would then have to be accepted onto the panel of other societies according to their own procedure for acceptance. Each society has different methods of assessing and appointing its judges. Judges can be removed from the panel for a variety of reasons, including any infringement of the rules, but in practice this happens very rarely. Judges are not allowed to judge any pony which has ever belonged to them or which has been stabled in their yard. They cannot judge their relatives' or business partners' ponies or children. Usually a judge will say immediately if he or she thinks that such a pony or rider has come before them – so don't try it!

The judge is, in effect, completely in charge of a class. Therefore you should not leave the ring after the class has started without asking the judge's permission (usually done through the steward). The judge can ask any pony to leave the ring if he or she feels that it is unsound or if its manners are unacceptably bad.

You must never, ever argue with the judge nor make any loud comments for the judge to overhear. It will do your reputation as a competitor or connection of a competitor no good at all. You can, however, approach a judge politely after the class has finished, if you are puzzled about any aspect of your marks. The marks will be displayed at the secretary's office after the judging of the championship (if there is one).

Judges and competitors must be unfailingly polite to one another. Neither must eat, drink or smoke in the ring. Judges should not read the catalogue, rummage in their handbag or pockets, or watch the class in the next ring whilst someone does their show in their ring. In novice classes, the judge should not wear a crackly plastic mac unless he or she wants mayhem, and mothers coming into the ring to remove saddles should not wear a strappy top and skimpy shorts to try and catch the eye of male judges.

THE MARKS

The marking system varies from society to society and from one class to another but most working hunter pony marks are allotted on the following basis. Around half the marks are allotted on a straightforward basis for the jumping round. A usual figure would be fifty marks out of a hundred. Marks would be deducted on a basis of ten for a knock down, fifteen for a first refusal, twenty for a second refusal and disqualification for a third refusal or a fall. There are also twenty marks allotted for style and jumping in this phase in British Show Pony Society classes. In National Pony Society classes the mark for style whilst jumping is only ten, with the conformation mark being correspondingly higher than the British Show Pony Society one, which is twenty. Other societies do vary slightly from this, so do check in your rule book.

Very occasionally, the steward will add up marks wrongly, sometimes effectively altering the positions which will, by then, already have been decided. If this happens and you can see an error in addition, you will have to bring it to the attention of the secretary. There are no set rules for dealing with his scenario and the show organisers will have to decide what action to take.

If you have jumped a clear round, then the only mark in the jumping phase that you can improve would be the style one. If you look at this mark on the result sheet and see that you have only got, for example three marks, do look at the marks of the other ponies. Every judge has his or her own way of allotting these marks and you might find that there is no mark above, say, five, in which case your mark is not that bad. If, however, there are marks up to eighteen, and you only have three, then you had better book some lessons.

Conformation marks are allotted according to the conformation of the pony, the freedom of his action (which includes straightness) and his type. You cannot really do anything much to change these aspects of your pony, although if he is in good general condition and well shod, he will be presented at his best. You may be puzzled to find that your pony's conformation mark varies wildly from show to show. You should, however, look at the other marks and see how he fares in comparison. Some judges mark high throughout and some mark low. There is also the element of the judge's personal preferences. If the judge just doesn't like your pony, he or she will mark him low throughout – you just have to accept that.

With mountain and moorland ponies, the conformation mark includes an element of whether or not the pony is a good example of his breed. Some judges favour one breed over another – this again is just the judge's preference and you cannot do anything to change this.

Wide disparity between the marks given to you by the same judge but at different shows is another situation that is difficult for some to comprehend. You could, for example, find that a judge will give your pony twenty-eight for conformation one week and then a couple of shows later, the same judge will give him only fifteen. This is not because one of your pony's legs has suddenly dropped off, rather it is a mark in comparison to the other ponies in the class on that day. If the ponies are very much the same ones as in the first class, it may be that your pony is not moving as freely as before or something like that. Most judges will not mind if you ask them politely when the class is over.

At the end of the day, you just have to accept the judge's decision, whatever the result, and if you cannot do this, you will never enjoy your showing.

CHAPTER ELEVEN

Class Procedure and Ringcraft

WORKING HUNTER PONIES

The first part of any working hunter pony class is the jumping phase, in which the ponies are required to negotiate a course of rustic fences. There will always be an opportunity to walk the course before the class, and, particularly for the inexperienced, this is very important. Course walking is always done on foot, so an attendant will be needed at the ringside to hold the pony. You should walk the route that you will be taking, memorising the order of the fences. If you walk more or less on the track that you will ride, you can see the approach to the fences as you will see them from the pony. Look at the striding between doubles and other combination fences, so that you will know what to expect. There is not usually a start and/or finish in a working hunter pony course, but just occasionally, a coursebuilder will put them in; if so, make sure that you go through both.

The fences will always look bigger from the ground and parents should be very careful at this stage not to put off younger riders. When a mother says, 'That one looks big,' or 'You will have to kick a lot here, dear,' it is guaranteed to set up a negative cycle of thought. This conveys itself to the pony and before you know it the rider and the pony have agreed to have a refusal at that fence. The parent who says that little Merrylegs always stops at the water ensures that he will carry on doing it every time! Also, beware of giving your child so many instructions that he doesn't know if he is coming or going – remember it is hard enough for adults to do everything right in the class, let alone children. Never, ever shout instructions from the ringside. Under most rules it will mean disqualification, and even if it doesn't, it will only distract a young rider.

There are, however, a few minor exceptions to this which can come under the heading of ringcraft. For example, if your child has difficulty in telling whether the pony is stood square in front of the judge, you can use a discreet hand signal to help him out. The same applies to a young child who has a tendency to canter on the wrong leg.

After all the competitors have walked the course, the first pony will go back in the ring to jump. Sometimes ponies jump in catalogue order, sometimes in numerical order, sometimes numbers are put up on a board by the ringside, but more often than not competitors sort themselves out. Check with the collecting ring steward if you are not sure which procedure to follow.

When it's your turn, ride across to the judge, either at a walk or trot (depending on the size of the ring or on the instructions from the ring steward) and halt in front of him or her. You will usually be greeted with a 'Good morning (or afternoon)' and you should reply accordingly. Normally you would not engage in any other conversation with the judge, but smaller children may be asked if they are sure of the course. The judge will then usually thank you, which is the signal for you to commence your jumping round.

If there is something really spooky on the course, it is often wise to trot past it on your way to the first fence to give your pony a preliminary look. Cradle stakes ponies should canter between the fences, but would be forgiven for a few strides of trot on a corner or when changing the rein. All other classes should proceed between the fences at what is called 'a good hunting pace'. This is rather a misnomer, because in twenty years of hunting, I seemed either to be standing still or galloping wildly – neither of which is right for a working hunter pony class! Possibly the best way to describe the pace required is to say that it should be a good strong canter, but without rushing or the pony pulling.

Sometimes a judge will ask competitors to finish their round with a gallop. This means that you should complete the jumping and then gallop on along the next long side of the ring, pulling up at the corner. If the judge has not asked for a gallop, just finish your round, return to the judge, coming down to a walk, then halt and say 'Thank you' and salute, before leaving the ring. If it is a big class, the next pony may well be sent into jump as you are finishing, and in that case you should just leave the ring.

Marking systems differ slightly according to which society's rules you are competing under, but a significant percentage of the marks are always allotted for the jumping phase. For this reason it is important to ensure that you do your best. Please refer to Chapter 10 for more information on how the classes are marked and for tips on improving your performance.

After all of the ponies have jumped, those with clear rounds, and possibly some of those who had only a few faults, will be called back into the ring, all together. This is the 'showing' phase and is conducted just like a ridden showing class.

At first all the ponies walk round the ring, one behind the other. Make sure that you have enough space between you and the ponies in front and behind you. Walk your pony on smartly and be sure that you have his attention. The steward will, at some point, instruct the class to trot on. You should always be alert and waiting for such instructions. It is no good realising that the others are trotting when several ponies have trotted past you, causing you to fall into trot in their wake. This looks very unprofessional. The same applies to the instruction to canter on. If your pony is at all unreliable about going on the right leg, try to start your canter in a corner and behind the judge, so that you can get the correct lead established before the pony is seen.

In some classes the steward will ask the riders to change the rein. This is done by trotting across the diagonal. Sometimes ponies will be asked to gallop on, along one of the long sides of the ring. When ponies are galloping all together, some get over-excited. If your pony is likely to do this, make sure that you gallop on your own, by getting into a big space before you start.

The ponies will then be brought back to walk, and the judge will ask the steward to call them into line. Keep your pony walking on smartly and stay alert. Remember to acknowledge the steward when you are called. When you arrive at the line, you must take your place next to the pony called in previously. On no account should you try to take a place further up the line or to push in between other ponies. Make sure that your pony stands squarely and that you have his attention, especially if you are near the top of the line and will be doing your individual show soon.

Each pony in turn will then be called forward to do an individual show. Some judges ask for a particular sequence or request that you trot towards them before you start. If there are no specific instructions, the pattern opposite would give you an opportunity to show off your pony's paces:

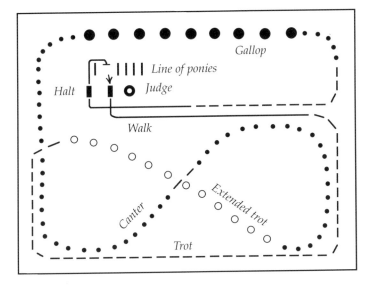

Gallop

Line of ponies

Halt   Judge

Walk

Canter   Extended trot

Trot

AN INDIVIDUAL SHOW

- Walk away from judge, in a straight line, towards the side of the ring.

- Turn right at the ringside and trot along long side in front of judge.

- Turn right and go up the side of the ring until almost level with the line of ponies.

- Turn right and go diagonally across ring, in front of judge, in extended trot.

- Canter on left rein in the corner of the ring. Canter half a circle, as shown, keeping in front of the other ponies.

- Change rein with a couple of trot strides and canter a similar half circle on right rein.

- Go behind the line of ponies and demonstrate your gallop.

- Come back to canter before the corner and then to trot, and finish by walking back to the judge.

- Halt smartly in front of the judge and salute.

- The judge will usually thank you. Return to your place in the line-up.

- Modify this show according to the size and shape of the ring.

Your helper removes the saddle and brushes off the saddle mark.

Sometimes ponies are also shown in hand. Your helper should be ready at the ringside and if he sees you dismount, he should come into the ring (taking care not to obstruct any other competitor who may still be doing a ridden show) and help you to remove your saddle. The saddle mark can then be brushed off and the pony generally tidied. If it is a cold day, a woollen quarter sheet can be put on the pony's back whilst he waits. On a wet day he can have a waterproof sheet and the rider can put a coat around his shoulders whilst he waits.

When all the ridden shows have finished, the first pony will be called out in hand. You should stand him up squarely in front of the judge and make sure you have the pony's attention. It is fine to gently rustle a sweet paper in your pocket or talk quietly to him. The practice of throwing handfuls of grass in the air is no longer a novelty to most ponies or to judges who get showered with it if the wind blows at the wrong moment. The judge will then thank you, and you should acknowledge him or her and move off away down the ring at a walk. Go about fifteen to twenty strides away from the judge, turn round, pushing the pony away from you, and run back towards the judge with the pony trotting. Go in a straight line which will take you just to one side of the judge and carry on trotting straight towards the side of the ring. Turn and go behind the line of ponies, and return to walk to regain your place. Your handler should then replace the saddle and leave the ring. You should remount. On a cold or wet day, the pony and rider can keep their extra layers

Waiting for your turn.

on until the last pony has gone out in hand, in which case the handler should stay in the ring and remove the rugs etc. at the last minute.

After all the ponies, or as many as the judge requires, have done their in-hand show, the class will be asked to walk on again and called in to their final placings. Remember, the judge is making his final decision and if things are close the way your pony walks out now could actually decide the class. Rosettes will then be presented and no matter where you are placed you should accept your lot with a smile! If you have any doubts at all about your pony accepting a rosette, hold out your hand for it and put it on your number string, rather than on the pony's head. If he is really bad about this, you must practise at home, because some judges will take a class away from a pony if his manners are unacceptable. The main prizewinners then canter a lap of honour and others leave the ring at a walk.

SHOW HUNTER PONIES

This is a purely ridden class, with no jumping phase. It is not usually judged on a marks system as such, but some individual judges, particularly when judging a big class, do ask their steward to write down a mark for each pony, to help them sort out the final line-up. Ponies enter at a walk, then proceed to trot and canter, just as in the working hunter pony class above. The larger ponies are usually galloped and the smaller ones keep this for their show. This is, however, not a hard-and-fast rule, especially when classes are not held under any particular society's jurisdiction, so your pony should be able to gallop with others. Always ensure that your pony is in his own space and is not 'covered up' by other ponies overtaking or getting in a bunch. If you have a problem circle away when you are behind the judge and go back into a bigger space somewhere else. You could also slow your pony down when going behind the judge, to create a bigger space in front of you, although this may cause the ponies behind to catch up.

The procedure is then exactly as in the ridden and in-hand sections above. Judging is done on the pony's conformation and type primarily. Type is important – for example, a Shetland pony with perfect conformation would not win a show hunter pony class – he is the wrong type. So a pony must first and foremost have good conformation and be of the right type. He must move correctly and be straight. His manners and way of going would be the next consideration. He should be obedient and forward going without pulling or going on too fast. Overbending, going with his head in the air and his back hollow, and similar faults would all be penalised. He should demonstrate a correct outline at all times. There should be no faults revealed by removing his saddle, such as a dipped back. Finally, the decision comes down

If you get behind another pony the judge cannot see yours.

to the judge's personal choice. You can't do anything about this at all. However, if you know a judge does not like your pony, there is not much point in showing under him or her again. Conversely, if a judge likes your pony, you can always look out for shows where he is judging. Be warned, though, you could still meet up with another pony which the judge likes better.

LEAD-REIN SHOW HUNTER PONY

Ponies come into the ring at the walk, led by a handler. The leading rein should be attached only to the back of the noseband. The lead rein should be held in the handler's left hand, with the pony walking on the handler's right, so that, if problems arise, the right hand can take a second, closer hold. The judge needs a full and uninterrupted view of the pony and rider, so the handler should keep to the outside so as not to obscure the judge's view whenever possible.

The ponies walk round the ring for a few minutes, then the steward will stop them in one corner. One by one, at the steward's signal, each pony will be trotted along the long side of the ring in front of the judge. When this part is over, all the ponies walk on again until they are called into line.

Individual shows are performed in walk and trot only, and would normally feature a trot on each rein, unless the judge gives specific instructions. Lead-rein ponies are almost never stripped.

STYLE AND PERFORMANCE

The ponies go in one by one and jump round a course of jumps, just as in a working hunter pony class. There is usually an area of the ring roped off for a second judge to judge the shows, whilst the jumping is in progress. Alternatively, if there is only one judge, the ponies come back in again, one by one, to do their show after all the jumping rounds have been completed. There is usually a set show for style and performance classes and this does vary slightly between the societies, but it will usually be printed in the schedule or rule book. If it is not, you will have to ask the show secretary. For practice purposes, a typical individual freestyle show might include the following movements:

- halt/walk on a long rein
- medium trot serpentine
- extended trot on the diagonal
- canter serpentine with changes of lead
- extended canter on the diagonal

As the name of the class suggests the emphasis is on the style of both the pony and rider and on the performance of the pony. The jumping phase will normally have smaller jumps than might be expected in an equivalent working hunter pony class, and there may well be fewer fences too. Concentrate on jumping a flowing round, keeping to an even pace and approaching the jumps in a calm, controlled way. Rushing at fences, trotting in places, napping to the collecting ring and other bad behaviour will all lose marks.

In the flat section, the movements are marked rather like a dressage test, with marks being deducted for disobedience, poor transitions, mistakes (in the required movements), uneven paces and so on. It should therefore be ridden just as you would hope to ride a dressage test.

The marks for the two sections are then added together, with no marks being allotted for conformation in this class, and the results are determined purely by the totals. If two ponies finish on the same mark, the judge will have to think back to the way the ponies went and give a plus or minus mark to one of them accordingly.

THE CHAMPIONSHIP

If your pony has been placed first or second, you may be eligible for the championship, if there is one. (The schedule will tell you this.) The first and second prizewinners from each of the height sections come together and basically do exactly the same

A championship presentation. Mrs Penny Priest presents a trophy to C. Ryder Phillips on Young Dragonara.

as the ridden part of the class, sometimes – but not always – including an individual show; it would be rare for a judge to strip ponies in a championship. Normally a second prizewinner would not expect to take a championship over the winner of his class or any other class. However, ponies do 'play up' and get over-excited in championships, so my personal opinion is that second prizewinners should always appear in the championship – you just never know with showing!

A FEW IMPORTANT RULES TO REMEMBER

Although the rules vary from society to society and year to year, there are some basic guidelines which apply.

- In **mountain and moorland** classes, the pony must be registered with the official breed society.

- In **National Pony Society** classes the pony must be registered in their competition record before it can compete. A height certificate is not required on registration, but if the pony qualifies for the finals, a certificate would then be required.

- In **British Show Pony Society** classes, the pony must be registered with the society and the owner and rider be members. All registrations have to be accompanied by a height certificate. Please check with the current rule book for the exact regulations covering height certificates.

- **Age:** Under all rules, ponies are required to be *at least* four years old, and in some mountain and moorland classes the lower age limit is five. For rules regarding age of rider and height of pony for your chosen class, always consult the current rule book.

- **Tack:** Generally any suitable bridle is allowed. The exception is novice classes where a snaffle bridle is usual. Tack may not be changed at any time after the class has started and the same tack must be worn in a championship.

- **Riders** are never allowed to ride more than one pony in a class. In a championship, a rider may be substituted, if the same owner has more than one pony eligible for that championship.

- **The course** will be set by a coursebuilder and no-one but him or her may alter the course in any way. No-one will ever be allowed to practise over any part of the course, before the class begins.

- **Outside assistance** from the ringside is not allowed. Connections of a pony should never shout encouragement or instructions.

- **Exhibitors and handlers** should never enter the ring without the judge's permission, unless it is to strip the pony, as described above.

- **Judging:** No pony should be shown under a judge who has either owned, bred, sold or produced that pony or had any previous connections with it. If you are in any doubt about your pony's previous history, it is better not to compete. Most judges will be very happy to speak to you after the class, so that you can find out for sure.

A superb gallop from Anna Evans on Sandpiper Bay.

CHAPTER TWELVE

The Working Hunter Pony Course

THIS WILL consist of rustic fences, usually not less than five in number, and supposedly of solid construction, but courses do vary dramatically from show to show. In a small ring there may well be fewer fences with less space between them, which does call for more concentration from pony and rider. A big ring with fences well spread out will encourage a flowing round, but smaller children may forget the course route. The height of the fences will be relative to the society under whose rules the competition is held, and to either the height of pony and the age of the rider, or in the case of mountain and moorland ponies, to the height or breed of the pony.

Although rules do call for rustic fences, you may encounter a wall or something similar that has been borrowed from the show-jumping ring, so be prepared for this. Most working hunter pony fences will be garnished with bits of greenery and these may hang partly over the fence.

TYPES OF FENCE

• **Upright:** This can be a single pole, cross-poles or planks. It may be a narrow filler underneath a single pole.

Generally, you should not get too close to an upright – judging your take-off point in front of the fence to be approximately equal to the height of the fence.

• **Spread:** This can either be a parallel, in which the back and front parts are the same height, or more usually it will have the back part of the fence higher than the front.

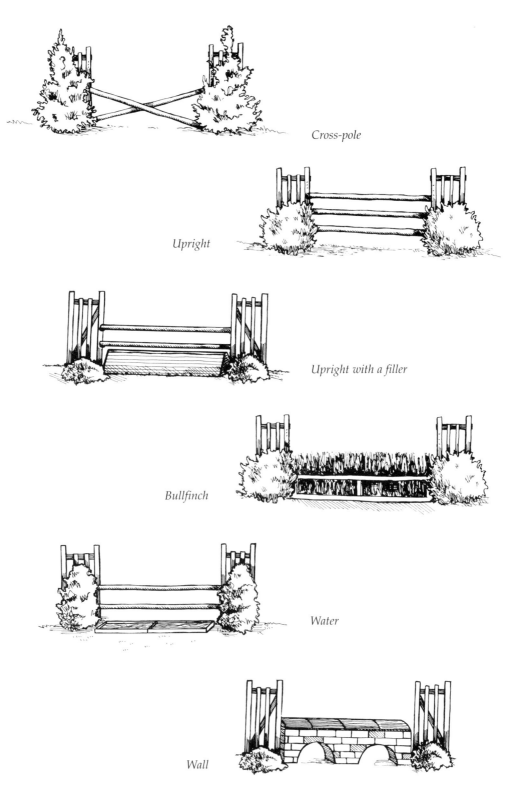

Cross-pole

Upright

Upright with a filler

Bullfinch

Water

Wall

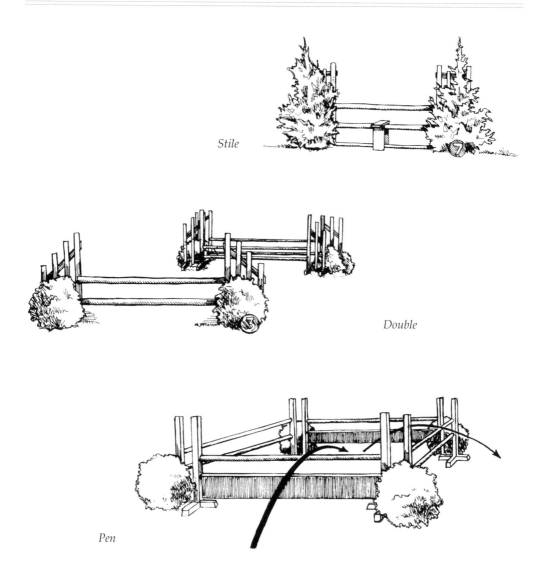

Stile

Double

Pen

Ponies jump spread fences well. In working hunter classes there might be a spread fence made up of a bench-type structure. Sometimes there are flowerpots or other decorations on the fence. To jump a spread fence, the take-off point is nearer the fence than if jumping an upright. There should be an increase in impulsion when approaching the fence. Spread fences with ditches, water trays or troughs underneath them look far worse to the rider than they do to the horse. Just look ahead and kick on!

• **Doubles and other combinations:** A pen is a favourite hunter pony jump. This means that there will be two doubles to jump, in different directions. If such a fence is well decorated with greenery, and the pony cannot see what he is jumping into, it may take determined riding to encourage him. Changing direction in a pen can be difficult and is a good exercise to practise at home.

The pony who has had a thorough education will cope with a bounce fence in the ring when he meets one. If you have a refusal at the second or later part of a combination, you have to go back and start from the beginning of that series of fences. If you have a refusal in a pen, you can attempt that part again. If you are eliminated, you will have to look for the steward's help in extracting you from the fence. Good practice is to build a pen at home and then jump it in different directions – turning right or left or going straight on – so that the pony does not get to think he knows best and just go straight on at this type of fence.

A stile can sometimes be used as the second part of a double. It can be offset to one side or the other of the previous fence. This calls for much concentration and good steering.

• **Water and other hazards:** The societies have different rules concerning hazards, but in general water is walked through – only being jumped over when in troughs or trays. Bridges and banks are also allowed and coursebuilders do like to take advantage of these natural hazards to enhance their courses. If you have a problem with ditches you will just have to dig one in your field to practise over. When not in use you could lie some large barrels on their sides in the ditch to prevent the pony falling into it when playing or when there is snow on the ground and he may not see it. The edge of the ditch should be delineated by poles, fixed firmly to the ground.

If you come across water which has to be jumped over, you will need extra impulsion to clear the width. However, you should not be travelling so fast that if your pony stops he will give you a bath.

• **Bullfinches and hedges:** If there is a natural hedge in the ring, it can be incorporated into the course, providing it comes within the height limits for the class. To train your pony to jump bullfinches you should start with a plain hedge and then gradually add branches of greenery, closing the gap in the middle until there is only the slightest thinning to show him where to jump through.

121

• **Nasty-looking fences!:** These would include jumps into a wood, over a drop or possibly into a river. An obedient and confident pony will do as he is asked. However, ponies with a brain will think twice about jumping a fence out of the sunny showground and into a dark wood with all sorts of unknown hazards, and may decide that discretion is the better part of valour. For these clever ponies, the best approach is probably fairly slowly, giving him time to look at what is going on. If your pony lacks boldness, you will just have to give him more experience. However, ponies should never be asked to jump blindly into a combination. On a recent course, ponies were asked to jump into woodland, from light into relative darkness, whilst negotiating a bounce to another fence. A bold pony jumped into the woodland and landed on the second part of the combination – luckily with no long-term damage, but nevertheless receiving a bad experience.

Course designer Alan Oliver's plan for the 1994 BSPS Championships.

A good coursebuilder will build a course that most competitors get round with few or no faults. He or she will alter the distances between combinations as the classes change, and will always keep within the height limit for the appropriate society. Jumps would not normally be built on rising ground, which can

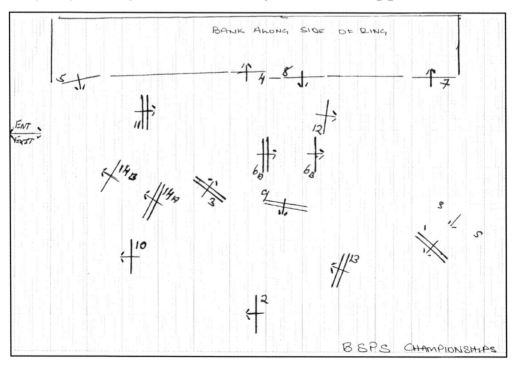

cause problems, and all course-building materials should be strong and safe. Any greenery should be well secured to avoid it falling or blowing down as a competitor approaches, and all unused cups should be removed.

A FEW JUMPING TIPS

Always watch how a course jumps for the competitors before you. If the distance looks a little short, for example, in a combination, you will know to come in on a short, bouncy stride.

If a corner appears sharper when being ridden than it did when you were walking the course, you will know to approach steadily and to take as wide a line as possible.

However, do not get into the 'me too' syndrome. If too many ponies stop at a particular fence, then everyone else starts expecting to stop at it and it becomes a 'bogey' fence. I know that horses are herd animals, but that is taking the herd instinct just too far!

To build a good course is an art – so be ready for the less-than-perfect course which you will meet every so often.

A lovely jump from Langfield Jamaican Ginger, ridden by Emma Williams.

Postscript

So WHY do many thousands of ordinary people, often not particularly well off, turn up week after week at shows all over the country? It is primarily for that one moment when everything becomes worth it, no matter what the cost or effort involved. The moment when the pony that you have worked on for hours, weeks and months, stands before the judge and is proclaimed champion. However, it is also about the cama- raderie between competitors – when, for example, someone rushes over to lend a hand when you are late for a class or gives you a lift in their lorry when yours is off the road; it is about the delicious horsey chat over a cup of tea when your class is over; and knowing that when your child grows out of his or her pony, you will probably already know someone who wants a pony that size, just as you will have had your eye on one in the next class up. You get to know the ponies regularly competing, just like you get to know the people.

Another advantage is that the pony who is shown gets a more interesting life than the one kept for hacking. He is usually trained to a higher standard, because his performance in the ring demands it. He is groomed and turned out to perfection, and it is very satisfying to do this job properly. The show pony gets to travel about and become accustomed to the sights and sounds of the showground, which must help to make him a safer ride at home. Many showing people will tell you that they do not mind where they come in a class, as long as the pony has gone well, and indeed it is a great pleasure to see your pony going round in the ring and to be proud of him. Winning is the real icing on the cake.

So if you want to show for the rosettes and cups, I would

advise you to go out and buy some. It is much cheaper and quicker. If you think you might make any money showing, forget it. Money is only made by professional producers and those lucky people who buy a young pony cheaply, show it successfully and then sell it for a great deal more than they originally paid for it. Even these people, if they were to count the time they had put in, would not feel they had made much actual profit. If you want to show your pony, so that you can give him an interesting life and train him to a standard that you can be proud of, then I'll see you in the collecting ring.

Good luck!

Useful Addresses

British Show Pony Society,
124 Green End Road, Sawtry,
Huntingdon, Cambs. PE17 5XA
Tel: 01487 831376

British Show Pony Society, Scottish Branch,
Bridgehill Farm, Harthill,
Shotts, Lanarkshire ML7 5TR
Tel: 01501 51257

Joint Measurement Scheme,
British Equestrian Centre,
Kenilworth, Warwickshire CV8 2LR
Tel: 01203 696620
Fax: 01203 696685

National Pony Society,
Willingdon House,
102 High Street, Alton,
Hampshire, GU34 1EN
Tel: 01420 88333

Ponies Association UK Ltd.,
Chesham House,
56 Green End Road, Sawtry,
Huntingdon, Cambs. PE17 5UY
Tel: 01487 830278

Index

Advertisements 25
Age (pony) 116
Arrival at show 98-102
Auction sales 24-5

Back 34-5
Barley 71
Bathing a pony 61-2
Bits 83-4, 89-90
Boots (pony) 87-8
Boots (rider) 91
Box walking 26
Bran 72
Breeches 91
Bridles 83-5
British Show Pony Society 8-9, 13-20,
   77-8, 93, 100, 104, 116
Browbands 84-5
Brushing 38
Buttonholes 91
Buying a pony 21-30

Cannon bone 33-4
Canter 44
Cavalletti 51
Chaff 72
Chamomile 75
Championship 115-16
Class procedure 106-17
Cleaning tack 88-9
Clipping 63-5
Clothing, rider's 90-2, 96
Colour, coat 39-40
Confidence 55-6
Conformation 24, 27, 31-41, 105
COPD 26
Course, jumping 106-7, 118-23
Cradle stakes 11-13, 107
Crib-biting 26, 80

Dandelion 74
Dishing 38
Double bridle 90

Elbow 32-3
Electrolytes 102
Equipment for show 94-7
Exercises 41-5, 47
Eyelash trimming 65

Fatness 39
Feeding 70-5
Feedstuffs 71-2
Feet 34, 75-6
Fences 118-23 *see also* Jumping
Fenugreek 74
First aid kits 96
Fitness 39, 57
Flatwork 41-5, 47
Forelimbs 33

Gallop 44-5, 107
Garlic 74
Girths 87, 89
Gloves 91-2
Grey ponies 62
Grid, jumping 52-3
Grooming 59-69; kit 59-61, 95

Hacking 47
Hair 92
Half-halt 47
Halt 45
Hay 70-1, 73-4, 90
Head 32; trimming 65
Heel trimming 65
Herbs 74
Hind leg 35
Hock 35-6
Hood 81

In-hand showing 110-11
In-hand training 45-6
Individual show 109

Jackets 90
Jodhpurs 91

Joint Measurement Scheme 77-8
Judges and judging 103-5
Jumping 49-58

Kelp 74-5
Knee 33

Laminitis 26
Leading rein classes 92
Lead rein pony of show hunter type 18-19, 113-14
Leg, trimming 65
Lorry 97-8

Management of the hunter pony 70-82
Mane 60-1, 66-8
Manners 48
Marks, judge's 104-5, 108
Measurement 77-8
Mint 75
Mountain and moorland ponies 39, 105; working hunter 8, 17
Movement 27, 36-8

Napping 57
National Pony Society 9, 17, 77-8, 93, 104, 116
Neck 32
New Zealand rug 81
Nosebands 85
Novice working hunter pony classes 16
Nursery stakes 13-14

Oats 71
Open working hunter pony classes 14-16
Overbending 46-7, 112

Paperwork 93-4
Pastern 34, 36
Pelham 89-90
Performance and style 114-15
Plaiting (movement) 38
Plaiting (mane and tail) 66-9
Ponies of Britain 8
Ponies UK 8, 13-20, 116
Pony Club 55
Presence 40
Provisions for show 94-7
Pulling a mane 66

Quarter marks 100-1

Refusing jumps 57
Reins 85, 89

Ringcraft 106-117
Rugs 81-2, 95
Rules 116-17 *see also* British Show Pony Society, National Pony Society, Ponies UK
Rushing jumps 56-7

Saddlery 30
Saddles 86-7
Scars 29
Serpentines 43-4
Shirt 90
Shoes 75-6
Shoulder 32
Shoulder-in 47
Show day 93-102
Show hunter pony 7-9, 18-20, 112-13
Showing in hand 110-11
Snaffle 89
Socks 61
Stable management 78-80
Stabling 78-80
Stinging nettle 74
Stirrups 87
Style and performance classes 18, 114-15
Sugar-beet 71
Supplements 74

Tack 30, 83-90, 95, 116; cleaning 88-9
Tail 35, 61, 68-9
Teeth 32, 76-77
Tidying mane and tail 67-9
Trailer 97-8
Training, basic 41-8; in-hand 45-6
Travelling 97-8
Trimming 65-6
Trot 43
Trotting poles 50-3
Turn-out 59-69

Vaccinations 77
Vices 26, 80

Walk 43
Water (to drink) 73-4
Weavers 80
Whiskers 65
Windsucking 26, 80
Wisp 60
Working hunter pony 7-9; classes 11-18, 106-12; jumping courses 117-23
Worming 76-77

Young pony 49-50